# Beside Every Successful Man

# Beside Every Successful Man

## A Woman's Guide to Having It All

## Megan Basham

THREE RIVERS PRESS

NEW YORK

Copyright © 2008 by Megan Basham

Published in the United States by Three Rivers Press, an imprint of the
Crown Publishing Group, a division of Random House, Inc., New York.
www.crownpublishing.com

Three Rivers Press and the Tugboat design are registered trademarks of
Random House, Inc.

Originally published in hardcover in the United States by Crown Forum, an
imprint of the Crown Publishing Group, a division of Random House, Inc.,
New York, in 2008.

Library of Congress Cataloging-in-Publication Data

Basham, Megan.
    Beside every successful man: a woman's guide to having it all / Megan
Basham.—1st ed.
    1. Housewives.   2. Self-realization.   3. Man-woman relationships.   I. Title.
HQ759.B36 2008
646.7'8—dc22        2008017479

ISBN 978-0-307-39364-7

Printed in the United States of America

*Design by Lauren Dong*

10   9   8   7   6   5   4   3   2   1

First Paperback Edition

*For Brian, who assures me that I could conquer the world
and then tells me I don't have to.*

# Contents

PROLOGUE: THE YELLOW ROSE OF TEXAS  1

INTRODUCTION: WHAT WOMEN WANT AND HOW THEY
  CAN GET IT  15

1  MEN, MARRIAGE, AND MICHELANGELO  35

2  HOW TAKING A STEP BACK CAN MOVE YOUR HUSBAND
  CLOSER TO THE TOP AND YOU CLOSER TO HOME  63

3  MOTIVATING YOUR OTHER HALF: TURNING APPLAUSE
  INTO PROFIT  93

4  YOUR SECRET SUPERPOWER: HELP ONLY YOU CAN
  OFFER  123

5  USING YOUR PR SAVVY TO INCREASE HOUSEHOLD
  CASH FLOW  145

6  HOW YOUR SKILLS CAN STILL MEAN BIG BUCKS
  EVEN IF YOU'RE AT HOME  171

7  KEEPING YOUR PERSPECTIVE AND ENJOYING
  YOUR LIFE  197

CONCLUSION: MORE THAN JUST A MARRIED WOMAN  211

*Resource Guide*  225
*Acknowledgments*  237
*Index*  239

# The Yellow Rose of Texas

I am not the sort of person who has spent her life surrounded by women who married well and while away their days considering upholstery swatches, shoe shopping, and discussing Mommy & Me classes over lunch. Whether friends or colleagues, the women in my circle have mostly been smart, productive, and ambitious types. They are accountants and teachers, executive assistants and nurses, lawyers and other professionals. What they all have in common is that they left school planning to spend most of their adult years working in their chosen fields and expecting to always derive a lot of satisfaction from their careers.

Yet several years ago, I started to notice that among many of us, as other areas of our lives expanded, the enjoyment we derived from our jobs began to shrink. A lot of it was tied up with how our lives outside of work were transforming. We went from grabbing a drink with friends or dining out with a date after hours to making meals, attending dance recitals, or visiting with family. And suddenly work began to seem more like an intrusion on our real lives rather than a vital part of it.

I believe many of us were secretly a bit shocked when, somewhere in our twenties or thirties, our conversations shifted from strategizing how to secure a promotion and a raise to wistfully expressing a desire to take some time—maybe only a few years, maybe quite a bit more than a few—to embrace a slower-paced, more graceful, family-oriented life. A, well, let's just say it—a more *feminine* way of life. For some of us, that desire arrived with marriage. For others, with children. And for some (more power to them) that moment never arrived at all.

But for those for whom it did arrive, we suddenly found that the activities we would have rolled our eyes at in college were starting to look appealing to us. Talking about it over coffee or at lunch, we all felt a little bemused by our new compulsions to devote hours to planning a pumpkin patch excursion or to scrapbooking our most recent family vacation. One day we woke up and finally understood the appeal of Martha Stewart and wished we had time to add homemade flourishes to our holiday tables or to plan elaborate dinner parties where we could take the time to bake our own custard tarts rather than grabbing a store-bought pie and a carton of ice-cream on the way home from the office. This was the superficial stuff. On a deeper level, we wished we had time to cultivate stronger connections with friends and relatives, and that we could enjoy memorable family events rather than trying to stuff them into the nooks and crannies of calendars blacked-out with work commitments. Mostly we wanted time to enjoy being wives and mothers.

The problem was that this way of life didn't seem feasible for most us. We all had a couple of friends—the lucky few—who could actually follow up their fantasies with action. But like most people these days, we were part of a two-income economy. Our roads just didn't seem destined to lead to those intimate, comforting stops many of our mothers and grandmothers enjoyed.

But then several of us found a way off the highway and onto scenic country roads. For one friend it was encouraging her husband to accept a new job for more money in a less expensive city. For another it was that second baby, the child-care cost for which canceled out her paycheck. For one, her husband's family business took off, making her comparatively small salary irrelevant.

And the rest of us gnashed our teeth in jealousy and assumed that we had no other options. Whether your husband earned enough to make your income optional was simply a matter of luck. But the truth is, we had more power to change our lives than we thought. We just didn't know it. We weren't aware that in fact we were much more equipped to find the work-life flexibility we craved than our mothers or grandmothers could ever have dreamed of. We just had to start looking at our dilemma from a new angle and to start seeing our marriages as our own little business enterprises and our husbands as partners in that enterprise. And we had to approach the challenge of getting out of the office the same way we approached getting into it—with a rock solid belief that we could accomplish anything we set our minds to and a strategy for success.

DRIVING DOWN THE highway from Phoenix, Arizona, to El Paso, Texas, staring out at miles of sand, scrub brush, and rock, I couldn't help thinking, "What have I agreed to?" A few weeks before, visiting the city that would become our new hometown and the NBC affiliate that would provide my husband's new job seemed like an adventure. But now, as I scanned through station after station of Spanish-language radio and contemplated what exactly his new salary—less than half of what he had been making before—would mean to our lifestyle, my optimism from earlier in the month started to feel as fragile and dried-out as the tumbleweed fragments that occasionally blew by my window. How could we live on so little? How long would I be able to stand the cramped, economical apartment we had rented for temporary housing? And what would I do with myself after 7 P.M. while my husband was getting rested for his 4 A.M. show call? (That answer would present itself quickly enough: eat McDonald's.) As we passed yet another billboard advertising the exit for a nearby Indian casino, I couldn't help wondering whether the faith I had invested in the man in the driver's seat next to me would prove to be a well-placed gamble or a total bust.

It had taken a lot of strategizing, worrying, and discussion to get us to this point. When I first met Brian, he worked in public relations for a nonprofit organization, but he'd held several different jobs before that. He had been a teacher, a barista, a grad student, and a stockbroker—all of this *after* graduating from college with a degree in broadcast journalism. Six months before our wedding I threw him a surprise party for his birthday. The theme was his storied professional past, and everyone had to bring a gift related to one of his former titles. At the time, like everyone else who knew him, I thought this was hilarious. I found it less funny once the honeymoon was over.

Before that, I thought of Brian's job-hopping as an insignificant side effect of the characteristics I was falling in love with. As someone who tends to be obsessed with "shoulds" and "supposed tos," I envied how unburdened he seemed by other people's ideas of what a career path should look like. And he was so intelligent, warm, and witty that no one—not even my extremely traditional, business-minded father—doubted he would do well once he settled on a direction. When Brian went the customary route and asked my dad for permission to marry me, we were both a little surprised that he didn't bat an eye before welcoming Brian to the family. Didn't, in fact, express any concerns at all. "I knew the first time you brought him to the house that he was the guy," my dad told me later that evening, "and I have no doubt that once he figures out what he wants to do, he's going to be wildly successful at it." It was the second part of that assurance, the "once he figures out what he wants to do" part, that would pose a problem.

We married in early November. By late May my newlywed glasses were wearing off and I found myself trying to choke back the impulse (often unsuccessfully) to nag him about his career goals. There wasn't much opportunity for advancement in his field, and though he worked hard on the job, he didn't seem to have much passion for it. This was what I said out loud. Internally I worried that he would never earn enough to allow me to step back from work for a few years (or even to cut back to part-time) once we had children. I worried that if anyone was going to lift us out of living paycheck to paycheck, it was going to be me. And though I could hear the voice of my women's studies professor piping up in my head (*Well, why shouldn't it be you?*), the prospect of it stirred in me a faint but growing bitterness.

The situation came to a head in July, when Brian was in the middle of a two-and-a-half-month vacation. His position with the nonprofit involved working with local high school districts, so his schedule closely mirrored theirs. This meant he had most of our first married summer off while I continued with my forty-hour workweek as a curriculum editor at a large university press. Even though he was still being paid during that time, watching him snooze away in our bed as I went off to work every morning irritated me. It irritated me even more when I would come home at lunch to find him watching television. The rational part of my mind agreed that he should be able to use his time off however he wanted, but something about the sight of him in his boxers on the couch infuriated me in a way that I couldn't explain to either of us. Unable to express what was really bothering me, I settled for starting fights about housekeeping.

Slowly the truth came out. I wasn't angry that he wasn't doing the dishes or laundry, I was angry that his job was so undemanding it left him available to do so many dishes and so much laundry. And I was angry that I didn't see him making any plans for a future where he would be compensated more and around the house less. And most of all, I worried that my own dream—having children and the financial freedom to be able to spend the majority of my time caring for them—would be dashed if Brian didn't find a dream for his career.

When my true fears finally came out during a particularly heated argument, Brian looked not only stunned but also a little hurt. He assured me that he didn't think the job he was in would pay enough to start a family either, and that he expected to do something that paid better eventually. He said he always knew that he would have to get more serious about that part of his life after we got married, and that maybe he had let his bachelor ways linger on a bit too long. A short time later he decided to take a friend up on his offer of a position at the finance company he had recently launched. He didn't really enjoy the work, but it paid far better than anything else he had done—six figures in a part of the country where six figures can go a very long way. Even better, as a thriving business it presented numerous advancement opportunities and the potential for a much higher salary down the road.

But while the money was nice, it didn't take long to see that this was no solution either. Now Brian was coming home from work grumpy and uncommunicative. He would stare at the new television in our new living room and grunt that he didn't feel like talking because he'd been on the phone with clients all day. He lived for the weekends and medicated his unhappiness with food. His mother told me it reminded her of when he'd been a stockbroker—the job he'd hated above all others. If anything, this situation, which I had pushed so hard for, was worse than our original conflict, because I saw it creating distance between us. And now instead of feeling angry, I felt guilty. We had kept up with the Joneses and my husband was miserable because of it.

Around that time my office book club started reading David McCullough's biography of John Adams. While everyone else was getting caught up in the relationship between Adams and Jefferson and Adams and Washington, I was fascinated by the dynamic between Adams and his wife. I couldn't help noticing that he relied on Abigail in almost every facet of his work. When he was unsure whether to enter into national politics, she counseled him; when he felt unfit to achieve his goals, she encouraged him; when he had crucial decisions to make, she advised him; and when the press and his adversaries challenged him, she rallied supporters to his side. And in the midst of all this goal-setting and strategizing they wrote each other intimate, teasing, and tender love letters that revealed the sweet partnership they had in all things.

"*This* is what I want!" I thought. And once the Adamses opened my eyes to it, I began seeing examples of it everywhere. A Nobel Prize–winning economist told an interviewer that his wife's input was the key to his genius. A Fortune 500 CEO revealed that his career was going nowhere before he met his other half. Even David McCullough told the crowd at an awards ceremony of his wife, "I wouldn't be here, I wouldn't have had anything like the life I've had or the writing life I've had, if it weren't for Rosalee, my editor in chief." I didn't know these women, but I felt that they were big sisters letting me in on a long-hidden secret that this notion that women are to be separate from their men in work—either separated by their own careers or separated by caring for children—was a sadly limiting and isolating arrangement. Instead, these women showed me that whatever else a wife chose to do, she could be a vital, interactive force in helping her husband realize his ambitions. With my newfound perspective, I would work with Brian to carve out a path where we would both realize our fondest wishes. I believed I already had a good notion how to start.

"Honey, what do you think about going back into broadcasting?" I asked. "You already have a degree in it and it clearly suits your skill set." It wasn't the first time I'd brought up this subject, and he answered as he always did, that he couldn't stand reporting. He simply did not have it in him to be the person shoving a microphone into the faces of parents who have just lost a child, couldn't live with the cynicism that comes from immersing yourself in murder, depravity, and corruption year after year. But this time I was not of a mind to let the matter drop. "Then what do you want to do?" I pressed. "What would you do if education, experience, and geography were no obstacles?" He looked sheepish, and I could tell there was something rolling around in his head even if he was embarrassed to share it with me.

After much prodding and antagonizing on my part, he admitted that for the last couple of years he'd been thinking about how much fun it would be to be a weatherman. Meteorologists were a part of the energy of the newsroom, but their role had a more positive focus. Sure, weather could get severe, but it was rarely the pessimistic "if it bleeds it leads" business that the rest of the news often is.

"Great!" I responded. "So why don't you do that?" Brian looked at me as if I'd just asked him why he didn't go ahead and become a cowboy, and began outlining all the reasons it wouldn't work. He had just turned thirty—a fairly advanced age for an industry that feeds on youth. Plus his degree was in broadcasting, not meteorology. He'd have to go back to school, and he didn't know how to begin trying to land a job in the field.

I saw his point—it did seem daunting. But I was so relieved to finally be in a position where I could imitate the women I'd been reading about. I could be the cheerful, confident one, able to make a sacrifice on his behalf, and shrug off such hurdles. This is what marriage is all about, I told him. We both had certain strengths and we would simply pool them to get him where he wanted to go.

Once the decision was made, our marriage took on a new dynamic. It was like we were starring in our own private feel-good movie. *A young couple fights for victory against all the odds!* I began researching universities that offered flexible programs in meteorology. Brian, who immediately became more proactive than I'd ever seen him, started knocking on doors of local stations to secure a weather internship (he was going to have to live with the shame of being the world's oldest intern, he said, laughing). When that was done, we put together a résumé tape of his on-air work. Then I put the skills I used at the office to work for him, searching the Internet for open positions, polishing and repolishing his résumé. I used everything from his stint in college as a Jungle Cruise Skipper at Disneyland to his experience giving corporate presentations to make him look like a good hire. I wrote cover letters tailored to each opening, and I took envelopes stuffed with résumé tapes to the post office every afternoon. In short, I did all the things that Brian, who was now taking graduate courses and interning three days a week in addition to working, didn't have time for. Three months later, as he had done so many times before in his life, my husband accepted a new job.

While interning in Phoenix he had been advised that, starting out, the best we could hope for was a weekend position in a small town no one had ever heard of. Instead, he landed the weekday-morning gig in the twenty-first-largest city in the United States. At the time, I was thrilled, if apprehensive. It wasn't New York or Los Angeles, but it was an impressive start. Well, it was an impressive start marketwise. Moneywise it was petrifying, even though it was still far more than we had been told to expect. I tried to sustain that adventurous feeling I'd had when we first embarked on this enterprise, but my resolve started faltering as reality set in. Our house was sold, Brian had signed a contract, and we were moving.

When I had still been in cheerleader mode, long before we loaded up the last of our belongings into a rented U-Haul, I'd burned a CD intended to help us embrace our new status as West Texans. It started out with Hank Williams's "Take This Job and Shove It" and moved on to Marty Robbins's yodeling a tribute to our new hometown, before maxing out in full campiness with "East Bound and Down" from the movie *Smokey and the Bandit.* Like all the songs I chose for the mix, Johnny Lee's "Yellow Rose of Texas," I figured, would provide a bit of good-natured amusement for us, the urban, modern-rock-listening couple. It was corny, twangy, and thoroughly country, and I expected we'd get an ironic kick out of singing along with the songs our grandparents had loved. But as I listened to Lee sing of a woman who helped her man pick up the pieces of his life and begin again, I couldn't stop myself from feeling inexplicably, ridiculously touched: *She's the diamond of the desert, she's the golden flower of spring, she's the yellow rose of Texas, she can make a man a king.* It was hackneyed and backward and chauvinistic, and for some stupid reason it was making me a little teary.

It's been almost three years since that dusty drive to El Paso, and Brian's enthusiasm for his field and our close partnership have persisted. It has been amazing to watch the man I once accused of being a slacker take double course loads semester after semester so he could finish his meteorological certification in half the time. His efforts are paying off.

After completing his program and officially changing his title from weatherman to meteorologist, Brian was offered a position on a morning show in Tucson, Arizona, a much larger market that brings us close to friends and family. His new job also has meant a new, and better, salary. The scary starting-over days are behind us now.

Unlike many of the couples in this book, we are still in the early chapters of our story. But in the few steps we have taken, they and others like them have been a constant support for me. I gained certainty from their examples when I wondered whether it was silly for me to be so interested in Brian's career, and I learned from them when I didn't know how to help him but could see he needed me. I began this journey because of these women. And since that first drive down our new road, there hasn't been a day that I wanted to go back.

# Introduction

## What Women Want and How They Can Get It

While writing this book, I continually returned to the question "Who is this information for?" Is it for the mother who wants to work less so she can spend more time with her children? (Polling shows there are a lot of you out there.) Is it for the woman whose man is a bit lost professionally and could use some assistance getting on track? (Unfortunately, statistics show your ranks are growing every day as well.) Is it for the woman whose husband is already doing well but would like to know how she can help him do even better? As far I'm concerned, it is for all of you and many more.

Yet, as I started working, I couldn't shake the feeling that the very idea of a woman taking the time to learn how to help her husband achieve his best in the workplace was somehow controversial. I had trouble with every chapter I began, sounding, as my husband put it, as if I were "playing defense," though I couldn't see any legitimate reason why I should. After all, don't most married people want to see their spouse do well? Isn't a large part of the point of marriage to support each other's aspirations? I figured anyone in a reasonably healthy marriage would agree with me. But I knew that didn't change the fact that by writing to *wives* in particular I was treading on some very thin cultural ice.

It's strange that we have come to a place in our society where a wife's desire to support her husband's career should raise anyone's ire. Strange that while we are expected to do everything in our power to give our children a boost in the competitive work world they will someday face, it is not acceptable for us to even entertain the idea of doing the same for our men. I know how some critics will respond: "Yes, but you didn't write a gender-neutral book showing *spouses* how to help each other become more successful. You wrote one for *wives*." And it is true—the fact that I think this topic holds far more interest for women than for men is inescapable. As to why I believe it, I offer you two stories.

## The Opt-Out Revolution

If you've ever spent any time watching the E! entertainment channel, you've probably noticed that it is to television what fast food is to a balanced diet—cheap, artificial, and with its incessant focus on celebrity gossip, fairly unhealthy. Among the network's many superficial offerings one of the most superficial is a program called *Dr. 90210,* a reality show that follows the lives of Beverly Hills plastic surgeons and the wannabe actresses and models who frequent them. It is the kind of guilty pleasure one might indulge in (as I was doing one evening) while trying to get through the boring chore of folding laundry. Suddenly in the midst of scenes about fake boobs and Botox, a serious and timely drama began to play out.

One of the handsome young surgeons on the show had recently married an equally attractive doctor of internal medicine. If ever a pair could legitimately lay claim to the title "power couple," these two were it. But something about their interaction suggested that she was less enamored with where their new life together was headed than he was. At times their conversation about mundane matters—how their day at work went, how to spend their weekend—seemed to grow inexplicably tense. They just didn't seem in sync. But as the show progressed, the reason for their disconnect became clear.

In this episode they were engaged in what is usually a very exiting newlywed adventure: shopping for their first home together. Their real estate agent showed them several properties, with one in particular catching the surgeon's fancy. It had a formal dining room, a gourmet kitchen, and bedrooms to spare, all complemented by a sparkling pool and a glittering view of the Los Angeles skyline. It was as immense and impressive as their collective credentials, and it was located in one of the most expensive zip codes in the country.

Yet instead of reacting the way viewers might expect—by getting caught up in the excitement of potentially owning this palace—the lovely blonde doctor's jaw was growing tight and her eyes were narrowing in wariness. She watched in silence as her husband surveyed every detail appreciatively and declared it "home." Later, at their apartment, the mystery of her reticence was revealed.

"I really want it. I think it's just perfect for us," he said. "But if we're going to make the mortgage, you'll have to keep working."

"For how long?" she asked, her face looking on the verge of crumpling.

"I don't know. Indefinitely, I guess." Her expression indicated that this was not the plan they had agreed on before their wedding day.

"But we talked about having kids. You said you were ready." At this her voice jumped a panicky octave.

"There's plenty of time for that."

"Yeah, if you plan to have kids with another woman there is," she snorted back. "I'm thirty-five."

What struck me most about this exchange between Drs. Jason and Jessica Diamond was that despite how different their lives looked on the outside from my own and those of the women I knew (none of us expected to be buying multimillion-dollar homes anytime soon), their conflict was the same. She wanted to start a family and at the very least cut back to part-time hours; he wanted a lifestyle that usually requires two full-time incomes. Forget the old feminist bogeyman of men forcing women to stay home barefoot with babies; *this* has become the marital argument of our age. When my friends and I (most of us in our late twenties to early thirties) get together, our talk often involves when and to what extent our husbands are going to help us extricate ourselves from the office, not "Why won't those Neanderthals let us work more?" Recent headlines suggest that women all over are having the same conversation.

A lawyer from New Jersey tells the *Courier-Post* that she dreams of quitting her job and "grocery shopping at noon on a weekday." She claims that most of the younger women at her firm share her sentiments. In the same story a twenty-nine-year-old woman—another doctor—shares that while she enjoys her job well enough, she "hates that she has to have it," protesting, "I want to be a wife and a mom. . . . I shouldn't have to be a doctor." And in their recent coverage of the so-called mommy wars, *USA Today* reported on a thirty-nine-year-old marketing director at an architecture firm who says she aches to be at home with her four-year-old son.

These are only a few anecdotes, but they reflect a growing trend. If you are a mom putting in a forty-plus-hour workweek that leaves you feeling exhausted and homesick rather than fulfilled, you are not alone. Polls from every corner of the country show that women increasingly prefer to devote more of their prime years to caring for their homes and children. In 2005, the research group Greenberg Quinlan Rosner found that only 8 percent of moms want to work 35 or more hours per week. The other 92 percent are split about evenly between desiring part-time jobs and desiring no job at all. The Pew Research Center's 2007 survey came back with similar findings—only 21 percent of mothers say they prefer full-time jobs, down 11 points since 1997. And Oprah Winfrey's informal online poll found that while most working moms say they envy their stay-at-home counterparts, very few of the at-home crowd feels the same. (Lest anyone argue that everyone would say they prefer to work less if asked, most research shows that the majority of fathers, usually in the 75 percent range, favor full-time jobs.) Even young unmarried women who have yet to experience the emotional pull of children firsthand are saying they intend to spend more time caring for a family and less time climbing a career ladder. In a 2005 study conducted among female students at Yale University, 60 percent said they planned to cut back their hours or stop working once they have children.

The only problem is, not all the women who want to take a time-out from their careers, whether that means working fewer hours or not working at all, feel able to do so. The Bureau of Labor Statistics may have found that 1.2 million more mothers are staying home now than did ten years ago, and that millions more have downshifted to part-time work. But they also found that most of them are affluent, well-educated women in their thirties.

In a 2003 *New York Times Magazine* article titled "The Opt-Out Revolution," reporter Lisa Belkin wondered why, after forty-plus years of advances in education, business, and politics, women still don't run the world. Or at least don't run half of it. Why, she asked, when half of all MBAs are earned by women, are only 16 percent of corporate officers female? And why do only eight Fortune 500 companies have female CEOs? She looked around at her own social sphere, Ivy League graduates with advanced degrees and intimidating résumés who are now at home with their children, and had a flash of insight: maybe women aren't getting there because they don't want to.

Belkin found that it wasn't just that women had begun stepping back from the workforce; it was that educated, experienced women—women who arguably have the most to gain from working in terms of status and compensation—had begun stepping back. What was more, the women Belkin spoke to told her that they didn't leave work because they ran into a glass ceiling, but because they ran into a "maternal wall." Once these highfliers had children, the idea of mixing motherhood with the boardroom no longer sounded appealing. And because their Ivy League circles had landed them Ivy League husbands, they could afford to simply "opt out" of full-time employment.

Unfortunately only those women on the high and low ends of the economic scale typically feel able to opt out. Women on the low end do so because what they would earn as unskilled labor isn't worth the high cost of child care. For women on the high end of the scale, the cause is obvious. Their husbands' incomes give them the flexibility to choose whatever lifestyle they want, so they do. But what about the vast majority of working mothers who are simply logging hours at a job (quite a different thing from its elevated cousin, "the career") but would opt out in a heartbeat if they believed it was financially feasible? Most of the advice for them has been of the moralizing, belt-tightening variety. *If you really love your kids, you'll cut coupons, forgo vacations, and buy your clothes off the clearance rack until you've budgeted tightly enough to quit!* There's nothing wrong with following such admonitions, but let's face it, there is something sort of grimly puritanical about them. That said, they're considerably better than the lectures many feminist pundits offer, which simply tell moms to shut their mouths, get their behinds back to the office, and stop wanting what they want, as professor Linda Hirshman did in 2006 with her book *Get to Work: A Manifesto for Women of the World.*

Neither approach, assuming as they do that moms are either indulgent spendthrifts or lazy parasites, offers women the hope and respect they deserve. And both approaches ignore a viable third road that was the natural solution not so long ago. It is a road that our grandmothers and great-grandmothers trod instinctively. And it is a road that enables a wife who wants to prioritize her time at home over her time at work to use all the wonderful talent, intelligence, and skill she possesses to help her husband get ahead. Not only does this approach offer mothers an exit strategy, it allows them to opt out without budgeting all the niceties out of life. Helping their husband realize his ambitions on the work front is the key that can unlock the career shackles of millions of women who long to realize different, but just as valid, ambitions on the home front.

## What Wives Want

The other reason women are far more likely to desire this information has less to do with how women are changing than with how men are. From movies like *Knocked Up, Failure to Launch,* and *High Fidelity* to the perennial loser George on

*Seinfeld,* the specter of the twenty- or thirty-something male slacker has become ubiquitous in pop culture today. We see these storylines constantly—the bright, with-it woman gets involved in with a lazy but lovable underachiever and conflict ensues. It is no coincidence that the narrative has become so popular—our entertainment is acting as a mirror to what's going on in many relationships today.

It's not just that women are doing better, it is that men are doing worse. They are taking far longer to grow up and get serious about their careers than their fathers and grandfathers did, with the result that women are leaving them in the financial dust. Census data reveals that one out of three men between the ages of twenty-two and thirty-four is now living at home with his parents, a 100 percent increase from twenty years ago. Not only are women far outpacing men in college enrollment, but vastly more go on to graduate—four women for every three men. And whereas women's inflation-adjusted wages have increased dramatically in the last thirty years, men's have decreased.

In fact, women have pushed forward to such a degree that in a number of metropolitan areas women in their twenties are now significantly outearning males in their twenties. In Dallas, for example, young single women make an average of 20 percent more than young single men.

This would all be great if women were happy with men who earn and achieve less than them. Unfortunately most of them aren't. As prominent sociologist Catherine Hakim noted about women's mating preferences, "Even the most qualified and high-earning women reject role-reversal in favor of a partner who is at least equal, preferably superior, in earnings, status, and power."

Among the many studies to prove this point, the largest of

its kind was conducted over five years with more than 10,000 subjects on six different continents. Researchers surveyed everyone from Americans to Aleuts to Mbuti Pygmies to find out what men and women are attracted to in a mate. What they discovered shouldn't come as a shock to anyone who's ever been on the dating scene. Though there are many traits both sexes find appealing, we differ on two major points: Men place a lot of importance on how a woman looks but care little about how much she earns or how prestigious her job title is. Women, on the other hand, don't place as high a premium on appearance; they are more concerned with finding a man they believe has a high economic capacity. This can mean someone who already has money and power, or it can just as easily mean someone intelligent, industrious, and socially skilled—someone who gives off indicators that he has good economic prospects.

After reviewing the results, which held true in all age groups in thirty-seven different cultures, an evolutionary psychologist who participated in the study was compelled to conclude, "These preferences cannot be attributed to Western culture, to capitalism, to white Anglo-Saxon bigotry, to the media, or to incessant brainwashing by advertisers. . . . They are deeply ingrained, evolved psychological mechanisms that drive our mating decisions." In other words, living in an age that champions rigid definitions of gender equality does not change the "gathering" part of our brains that seeks out and responds to the "hunter."

During the time that I was wrangling with every chapter in this book—stopping, scrapping, and restarting in intermittent fits—my husband challenged me with this question: "Why did you really become interested in this subject?" After I intellectualized about women's polling data and economic theory for a few minutes, my true motivation tugged at a corner of my mind. I'm writing it, I told him, because of a couple we knew during those early days of our marriage that I feared we were on the road to becoming. They were a wonderful, charming pair, and everyone who knew them loved them. So it was a shame, both for them and their three-year-old son, when they decided they couldn't go on loving each other.

Vanessa* met her husband Nick* in high school. He was smart, funny, and articulate, and it was easy to see why she fell for him. They married early, while they were both still in college. But though their personal lives were intertwined from that point, their professional paths diverged immediately. A go-getter from early in life, Vanessa graduated from college with honors and quickly went on to earn a master's in business administration. By thirty-five she had held executive positions with two different companies. But while she was finishing grad school at the top of her class, it took Nick seven years of sporadic attendance to earn a liberal arts degree in a subject that no longer interested him. He then tried his hand at various careers, but he never found one that sparked any initiative in him. This isn't to say he did nothing. Rather, he drifted through several mid-level positions, moving when necessary to advance his wife's opportunities. As a result, his earning power was quickly no match for hers.

After a few years Vanessa began to experience gnawing dissatisfaction. It wasn't just that Nick didn't make a lot of money, it was that he never talked about having any goals or plans for the future. She hated feeling like the only responsible adult at home and took to nagging Nick about his work. He screamed that he already had a mother and didn't need another one.

* Names have been changed.

It might have ended then, but because of her spiritual convictions, she determined to stick it out. So they went to marriage counseling, learned to be more demonstrative, and became more in tune with each other's emotional needs. But not once during those sessions did she bring up what was really bothering her. "I just didn't know how to say it. Tell your husband that you wish he had a better job or at least some ambition for a better job? It would have been too mean to say."

The therapy helped enough to get them through another two years, until their son was born. And then the thing that seemed "too mean to say" became an elephant in their living room. The affectionate, teasing couple we all knew started looking tense at dinner parties. She finally confided to me one afternoon, "You know, I realized when I was looking over my company's new health insurance plan and trying to figure out how much it would cost to keep Nick on it that if I stay with him, this will be the dynamic forever. I will always feel like I'm married to a boy that I have to take care of. I think I'd rather be a single mom."

Despite the lofty ideals she'd once held that it didn't matter who was bringing home the bacon as long as someone did, she resented her husband's lack of drive and income until neither one could stand living with her disappointment another day.

Vanessa's reaction to being her family's financial provider is not unusual. In an article for msn.com titled "The Secret Lives of Breadwinner Wives," columnist M. P. Dunleavey voiced the discomfort many women experience from being the spouse with the bigger paycheck: "To the outside world, we probably look like the storybook version of a spunky female career gal who falls for the supersmart artsy guy—and together (cue the harps and a nice big sunset) they make it all work! But in reality, I guess I was kinda sorta hoping this arrangement would be temporary." Dunleavey's chagrin at the position she found herself in still seems relatively mild. And perhaps it will stay that way. But if so, she's in the minority.

When *New York* magazine talked to divorced women and family therapists about the toll this arrangement can take in every area of a couple's life—especially their sex life—their description was a bit starker:

> According to psychologists (and divorce lawyers) who see couples struggling with such changes, many relationships follow the same pattern. First, the wife starts to lose respect for her husband, then he begins to feel emasculated, and then sex dwindles to a full stop. . . .
>
> "Sexuality is based on respect and admiration and desire," says Anna [a woman who earns considerably more than her ex-husband]. "If you've lost respect for somebody, it's very hard to have it work. . . . Sex was not a problem for him," she goes on. "It was a problem for me."

Perhaps because my own parents modeled a more traditional arrangement or perhaps because I didn't have my friend's lofty credentials, I took a different road. Like Nick, my husband was smart, funny, and almost universally well-liked (in fact, people often commented on how similar they seemed). Like Nick, he was very easygoing and didn't seem to know what he wanted out of his work life. But I just could not believe that some part of Brian, with his many talents, didn't long to pursue a big dream, didn't harbor some vision of greatness. It took some time, but I eventually discovered that what I interpreted as a nonchalant attitude toward his career was really insecurity. For both our sakes and for the sake of our union, I decided I was willing to endure almost any risk to help launch him into a field he could feel ambitious in.

There is no comfortable way to couch this fact: it's hard for a woman to feel attracted to and in love with a man she doesn't feel is taking care of her. Most divorce research shows that when a woman makes either an equal amount as or more than her husband, she is more likely to leave him. Not just more likely to *experience* divorce, but more likely to find the marriage unsatisfactory and *initiate* divorce. For men the trend is the opposite. Contrary to what a few star-studded headlines might lead us to believe, a man who makes the larger part of the family income is statistically very unlikely to divorce his wife. As his earnings increase relative to hers, he is happier in their relationship and more committed to his family, making the marriage more stable. His wife is happier as well.

In a groundbreaking study out of the University of Virginia, sociologists found that women experience greater joy in marriage as well as greater overall life satisfaction when their husbands earn at least 68 percent of the household income. Even women who describe themselves as feminists are happiest when their husbands bring home two-thirds or more of the family's income. "I was very surprised to find that even egalitarian-minded women are happier when their marriages are organized along more gendered lines," said W. Bradford Wilcox, one of the study's authors. "Regardless of what married women say they believe about gender, they tend to have happier marriages when their husband is a good provider," he noted.

As women in an age where sisters are supposed to be "doing it for themselves," we can tend to feel a bit sheepish or even guilty for wanting men who are able to take care of us financially. But research suggests that we girls (or at least most of us) can't help it.

## The Beside-Every-Man Solution

Of course, there are other reasons for helping your man achieve his professional dreams that have nothing to do with wanting to be a mother or wanting your husband to provide well for your family (love jumps most readily to mind for me). Some of you might be looking for an outlet to use skills that don't get much exercise anymore. Others of you might long to feel more connected to your husband and hope that being more involved in the enterprise that takes up most of his weekday hours will bring you closer together. And some of you might simply have your eye on new furniture or a vacation home at the beach (hey, nothing wrong with that!). Whatever the reason, you can achieve all these goals by partnering with your husband in his.

There is a reason that the old adage "Behind every successful man is a good woman" became conventional wisdom. Throughout history a man who attained a high career status often had a woman (usually, but not always, his wife) to thank for helping him get there. Abigail Adams never won an election, yet her importance to our nation's founding cannot be overstated. When we hear the name Alfred Hitchcock, his wife Alma doesn't immediately come to mind. But without Alma, it is unlikely that many of Hitchcock's greatest films would have made it to the silver screen. And professional sports might look very different today had Rachel Robinson not given her all to support her husband Jackie. The idea that the only contribution women like these made was to keep the home fires burning is ridiculous.

Abigail Adams was a consummate diplomat and networker who worked tirelessly to further her husband's political agenda—which only makes sense considering she helped set that agenda. Alma Hitchcock collaborated with her husband on every aspect of his films, including scripts, casting, and editing. According to the couple's daughter this was an ideal arrangement for Alma, because she "accomplished the work she loved without having to deal with the rules and pretense of the so-called Hollywood life." Rachel Robinson was keenly aware of the stakes of her husband's success on the baseball field. She felt that, as a team, they owed it to the black community to break the color barrier of professional sports and used all her persuasive powers to keep her husband going in the face of crushing odds. These women all possessed valuable skills and immense talent, which they used to benefit their men and, by extension, themselves and their families. They didn't subvert their own gifts by helping their husbands, they magnified them.

Even if women today find this kind of partnership appealing, there is a sense that it's no longer an option. *But what about your career?* is the question friends and family members are likely to ask if you even mention it (as though we have only a finite amount of talent and can't afford to expend any on our husbands' goals). Or we've been taught that working or staying home is an either/or proposition. Either you're using your skills and education to further your own career or you're not using them at all. What we have lost sight of is that many men still get to the top of their fields in part because their wives perform tasks and take on responsibilities out of love that anyone else would be paid for.

Billionaire investor and Citigroup CEO Sandy Weill unequivocally states he would not be where he is today were it not for his wife's assistance, as does Richard Parsons, CEO and chairman of Time Warner. Thousands upon thousands of men who haven't graced the covers of *Forbes* and *BusinessWeek* but are successful all the same say likewise. They report that their wives' advice, actions, and attitudes gave them an arsenal of professional weapons that other men did not have, and that their efforts helped them jump to the front of the pack.

Yet despite the fact that so many high-achieving men continue to sing the praises of their wives, we rarely hear from these women. Business reporters talk to everyone from former professors to current colleagues to find out how a certain man became successful, but almost no one talks to the person the man himself gives credit to. This is a shame, because women today are, if anything, more equipped to help their spouses succeed than women of previous generations were. Armed with more education and more applicable experience, all they need is for someone to assure them that not only is it possible to do so, it is okay to do so.

There is a reason this book is titled as *beside* every successful man rather than *behind* him. It is about your taking the best part of the progress women have made and combining it with age-old wisdom to create a more satisfying future for both you and your husband. The wives who were the models for this book are not put-upon "little women." They didn't abandon their own ambitions and desires by helping their husband achieve his. They fulfilled them. Their service isn't the same thing as *subservience*—they stand beside their husbands as equal partners.

Nor are these wives scheming Lady Macbeths, prodding their miserable men down paths they never wanted to take. The men they are married to are, by their own admission, more fulfilled because of what they have accomplished and happier in their marriages because they know their wives value and respect their work.

This book is about real women who practiced simple though sometimes challenging principles to help their husbands achieve results that benefited their entire family. As I looked at each of them, I realized that they didn't just perform action that exhibited one or two of the principles. They performed action that exhibited *all* of them. It was difficult even to assign them to chapters. Wherever their husbands were on their career path—some in retirement after a great run, some just beginning to see their efforts pay off—almost every woman provided a strong example for each.

Finally, this book is not about judging women for what they want to do with their lives. I think we have had enough of that. We are all different, with different priorities and goals. And I believe most of us are tired of being lectured to and belittled for having those goals by people who know nothing about our daily lives. So what you are about to read won't tell you what you *should* want. It will tell you how to get what you *do* want.

# TAKEAWAY FACTS TO ENCOURAGE YOU

1. If you have secretly longed to leave your full-time job behind in favor of homemaking or child-rearing, you are not a pathetic 1950s throwback, you are not lazy, and you are not alone. Despite what you may hear in the media, many women feel the same way you do. Even women in the most prestigious careers. There is nothing wrong with women who *want* to reach the top of the corporate ladder or see their name in lights. But there is also nothing wrong with you—you aren't betraying any other women by following your heart.

2. There is a way to opt out *and* improve your family's economic prospects.

3. Wanting a husband who takes the lead in breadwinning does not make you a gold digger or a leech. Throughout time, all over the world, in every culture, women have felt this way. It doesn't mean we should behave like opportunistic shrews, but it does suggest that being attracted to men who are able to take care of us financially is our natural instinct.

4. Marriages in which the husband earns two-thirds or more of the household income are the happiest marriages. They are also the marriages least likely to end in divorce.

5. All the skills, education, and experience you have acquired throughout your life do not have to go to waste just because you cut back on your career. There are infinite opportunities to use them and your natural gifts on your husband's behalf. Doing so can be the key to getting you both the life you want.

# Men, Marriage, and Michelangelo

ome of you may not need any further background information before diving into the action-oriented portion of
this book. You're on board, you have no doubts that you
can help your husband succeed at work, and you're ready to
move on to learning how. If you are one of these readers, you
can probably bypass this chapter, which explores the scientific
support for being the woman beside the man, and go straight
to the "hands-on" sections. (Though if you do you will miss out
on a lot of fascinating information about how men relate to
the different worlds of marriage and work.)

Others of you may be more like me and have a more skep-
tical nature. Whenever I pick up a book whose aim is to give
advice, I want to see hard evidence that backs up that advice.
It's all well and good that a particular approach worked for
the author and their case studies, but that's no guarantee that
it will have the same effect in my life. I want to see the
"macro" proof behind the "micro" examples.

If you're with a man who has always seemed unmotivated
and uninterested in succeeding professionally, you may understandably question whether anything you do can change
that. By the same token, if your husband is doing okay without your help or possesses much more education and experience than you, you may doubt that you have much to offer.
Or maybe you're just a really busy mom, and you need some
convincing that adding the task of helping your man's career
to your already full plate is worth your time. If any of those

descriptions sound familiar, this chapter is for you. It will provide your inner skeptic all the confidence she needs to move forward.

## The Magical Marriage Premium

When men in high positions claim in an interview or speech that they wouldn't be where they are today without their wives, it's easy to dismiss their words as lip service. A cynical person might even assume that the men are just trying to score points at home with a bit of empty flattery. But statistics prove that the credit such men give their wives is true not just for them but for most married men. Economists have found that after a man gets married, he immediately begins to earn more than he did as a bachelor—often without doing any additional work. They call this phenomenon the "male marriage premium."

Let's say Larry and Moe have the same job and the same level of education and experience, and work the same number of hours with the same results. The only difference between them is that Larry is married. Statistically, Larry will earn considerably more than Moe—as much as 20 to 50 percent more. In terms of real dollars, this means that while Moe makes only $50,000 annually, Larry is making $60,000 or even $75,000. That is the power a wife just naturally has on a man's income.

For over thirty years economists have studied the marriage premium, trying to figure out what causes it. They know that married men in some demographics accrue more of a premium than others, but no matter how they parse the data—young men, old men, college-educated men, blue-collar workers—they continue to find that husbands have a significant earnings advantage over bachelors. What they haven't always agreed on is why.

Some have argued that the disparity is caused by selection (the married higher earners were good catches to begin with), others that it is caused by discrimination (employers favor guys who have "settled down"), and others that it is the result of specialization (after men get married they don't have to waste time with housework, so they do better at the office). Yet each of these theories has eventually been disproved.

Selection can't explain the marriage premium because even when men aren't particularly good catches, they still go on to earn more after they wed. Young, uneducated "shotgun grooms" (meaning those who were pressured down the aisle because of an unplanned pregnancy) accrue almost as much of a premium as older, professional men who were considered hot prospects on the marriage market. And the fact that the premium appears to have a kind of compound-interest effect—the longer men are married, the larger the income disparity between them and single men becomes—also throws a wrench into the selection argument. The data suggests that whatever aspect of marriage it is that gives husbands a moneymaking edge, over the years it grows stronger.

Discrimination can't account for the premium either, as self-employed married men experience just as much of a premium as men employed by others do. And many women who remember how their husbands lived before their wedding day will instantly see the flaw in the specialization theory (the one that says husbands do better at work because their wives clean up after them). As a rule, single men don't do much housework. Time-use studies show that husbands and bachelors spend about an equal amount of time on household chores (read that as a *small* equal amount). So rather than suddenly hanging up their dish towels after they get married, men simply adjust to living in a cleaner environment.

This means that something a wife does—something more than cooking and cleaning—makes the difference. On this point, not only does economic research prove that having a wife causes a man to earn more than he would alone, it also proves that the behavior of his wife affects how *much* more he will earn.

As a woman's working hours increase, the amount of marriage premium her husband reaps decreases. One study found that men whose wives aren't employed earn an average of 31 percent more than single men, but for men whose wives have full-time jobs, that number drops to 3.4 percent. Other research has shown that the premium disappears altogether when a man's spouse works full-time. Recounting these results isn't done to make women who work feel bad about their jobs or to suggest that they can't also follow the principles outlined in later chapters to have a positive impact on their husbands' work. But it is to show that your interest in your husband's success and your availability to help him have a direct impact on his performance.

The assistance wives offer their husbands to create a marriage premium is often unconscious (though when it becomes conscious, the results are dramatic). It happens when they give advice during a dinner table discussion about something that happened at the office. It happens when they offer their husbands a sympathetic ear and a pep talk after a bad day. And it happens when they accompany their spouse to business-related functions and help form those all-important social connections. Understandably, the fewer hours a wife works and the less demanding her own career is, the more time and mental energy she has to devote to these things.

Among many studies following this trend, one of the most convincing was conducted by Frieda Reitman of Pace University. After tracking the careers of 231 men with MBAs, Reitman found that those whose wives did not work earned 25 percent more than those whose wives did. Reitman told the *New York Times*, "The traditional family men were on a fast track, with the highest income, jobs at higher management levels and greater pay increases, on a percentage basis, over six years." This could also explain why 80 percent of chief financial officers have stay-at-home wives. Not, as some have argued, because they can afford to, but because their wives have both the incentive and the time to support a husband's career, thus enabling him to become a chief financial officer.

Though the effect marriage has on men's earnings is persuasive in itself, perhaps the clearest evidence that you have unique power over your husband's income potential is how the marriage premium impacts women's earnings. To that the answer is simple—it doesn't. Married working women accrue almost no marriage premium regardless of how much or how little their spouses work.

At first glance, this seems unfair. Two working spouses usually offer each other advice, encouragement, and a social wingman, so why are men the only ones to realize a premium? While it is true that part of the marriage premium can be attributed to a wife's efforts, the other part of it probably lies in the fact that men typically have a different psychological attachment to work than women. This is especially the case after they become husbands and fathers.

## Men and Work

In 2002, Shaunti Feldhahn, a Wall-Street-analyst-turned-author, was just beginning work on a new novel. One of the main characters in this work of fiction was a man, and she was having trouble writing him so that he felt authentic. She'd mapped plot points and planned what kind of obstacles he would face, but she couldn't quite get inside his mind to know how a man, and in particular a husband, would feel in certain situations. So she began to pick the brains of the men in her social circle to find out how they felt about love, sex, marriage, and all the other things that would play into the life of her protagonist. After listening to their responses, she had what she describes as a "lightbulb-on" moment: "I discovered that there were many things I thought I understood about men but really didn't. In several areas my understanding was purely surface level."

A lot of writers might have taken their newfound insights, completed their story, and left it at that, but Feldhahn possessed unusual qualifications for a novelist. Boasting a bachelor's degree in economics from William and Mary and a master's in public policy from Harvard, she wanted to make sure that what she was hearing from her male friends and family members squared with what men thought in general—she wanted hard data. The only problem was, she couldn't find any. This was strange, because if there's one thing someone who has served on the staff of the U.S. Senate Banking Committee knows how to do, it is find information.

Dismayed, she called her friend George Gallup Jr. of the famous Gallup Organization to ask him why she couldn't locate any polls on men's attitudes about their lives. "That's easy," Gallup responded. "Because there's nothing out there." Though literally hundreds of surveys ask women how they feel about being mothers, wives, and employees, few polling companies have bothered asking men the same kind of questions. Feldhahn thought this was a shame, because as surprised as she was by some of the revelations she'd heard, she figured other women might be as well. If she could prove that what she had learned about men on a small scale was also true on a wide scale and gather that proof into a book, who knew how many women would want access to that information? (As it turned out, a lot.)

To ensure that her results were as accurate as possible, she enlisted the expertise of a man named Chuck Cowan, the former chief of survey design at the U.S. Census Bureau. Together with another company called Decision Analyst, Cowan and Feldhahn conducted a blind random poll of four hundred men of all ages, ethnicities, and backgrounds. When the results came back, Feldhahn not only confirmed what she'd heard from the men in her life, she found that she had uncovered other common male experiences that the average wife probably isn't aware of—or if she is, she may not grasp how profoundly men are affected by them.

One of these surprising findings was the fact that most men have a different and much deeper relationship to their jobs than most women. As we saw in the introduction, ask a group of mothers if they would continue to work full-time if they didn't have to and the answer will overwhelmingly come back "No!" But when Feldhahn asked men if they would still feel a compulsion to keep working even if their wives earned enough money for them to live comfortably,

78 percent said yes. Even further, half the men revealed that when they put in long hours, it was by choice, not, as the majority of women report, because of pressure from employers.

It would be easy to dismiss Feldhahn's results if they were alone, but they are backed by two other sources as convincing as they are dissimilar—one of the most recognized and respected market research companies in the world, the other a website trafficked by millions of men every month that is as likely to ask visitors to rank beer commercials as it is to ponder the uniqueness of male priorities.

In 2007, the nonprofit, nonpartisan Pew Research Center conducted a national survey of parents that returned results almost identical to Feldhahn's. While only 20 percent of mothers said they would work full-time if they had their choice, 72 percent of fathers reported that they would. Meanwhile, when AskMen.com, the most popular men's site on the Internet, polled 72,000 of their readers on whether they would continue working if they became independently wealthy, three out of four said yes, they would either continue on their current career path or start another business. This is particularly significant given the findings of a 1955 poll on the same question. With a majority of about 80 percent, men then also said yes. So for all the political and social upheaval America has experienced in the last fifty years, the number of men who say they would be comfortable not working or staying home to raise children full-time has only increased by 2 to 8 points.

The pull men feel toward paid work regardless of their circumstances is surprising enough, but even more surprising is how often men think about their responsibility to provide for their families. In Feldhahn's survey more than two-thirds of the men reported that it is *always* or *often* on their minds.

Some have argued that this is because wives place unfair expectations on their husbands to earn more than their fair share of the family income, but this was not what Feldhahn's research bore out. "In my interviews I was startled to hear the explicit mental certainty most men had about their role as the family provider," she explains. "Whatever a man's wife felt about it, whatever she did or didn't earn, he felt that providing was *his* job. Period."

Though Feldhahn may have been the first, or at least the first in a while, to conduct a general survey on men's feelings toward their work, another researcher had been following the work attitudes of a specific group of men for years. Focusing his investigation on successful men—that is, men who had attained at least managerial-level jobs with upper- to upper-middle-class lifestyles—Robert S. Weiss, senior fellow and emeritus professor of sociology at the University of Massachusetts, also discovered that men see it as their duty to support their families regardless of how much income their wives bring home.

When Dr. Weiss's female staff first began receiving the responses from their study of successful men, their initial reaction was that something must be wrong; the participants must not be representative of men as a whole. After all, they knew plenty of men—they had fathers, brothers, boyfriends, and husbands—and none of them, they insisted, fit the profile for what they were seeing. The men they knew didn't identify themselves by their jobs as much as those in this sample, and they certainly didn't hold such traditional views of gender roles. Even Weiss was surprised, but for a different reason. As he quietly reviewed the interview transcripts, he realized that what he was seeing in the answers was himself. Because he'd never come across much evidence in the media or in conversation that other men were like him, he had always assumed that his preoccupation with his career and his feelings of obligation toward his family were unique. But as the study progressed and more transcripts came in, the responses remained the same. It became increasingly clear that these men *were* representative of their sex. "We are all cut out from the same cookie cutter!" Weiss exclaimed to his wife once the realization of how much he shared with his study subjects dawned. As it turned out, Weiss and his team, like Feldhahn, just didn't know men as well as they thought they did.

Despite the fact that two-thirds of the men in Weiss's study had wives who brought in some kind of income, the men still saw their roles as fundamentally different. "This view follows from their understanding of themselves as the marital partner ultimately responsible for the support of the home," Weiss noted. Even when their wives earned half or more of the family income, he found that the men saw "their own work as 'family-relevant' in a way their wives' work [was] not." With only two exceptions out of eighty (both of whom didn't yet have children), they "understood themselves to be the marital partner in charge of assuring the family's income.... The men might need their wives to help out if the household was to attain an aimed-at standard of living, but that did not diminish their responsibility for the domain. . . . If he accepted that the family's income was inadequate, the failure would be entirely his."

This doesn't mean that men don't consider their wives' work valuable or that they begrudge their having a career. It doesn't even mean that they don't appreciate the additional income—ask most men whose wives work and they will say it is nice not to have to bear the burden all alone. But that's just it: when the chips are down, they feel it is *their* burden. Yet, strangely, it is also a burden that—when they believe they're bearing it well—brings men great satisfaction with their lives and themselves. In fact, contributing less than half of the household income can cause men to exhibit psychological symptoms like depression and physical symptoms like headaches. The author of one of these studies published in the *Journal of Marriage and Family* discovered that this is true even when husbands don't have traditional views on gender roles: "Despite increasing support for nontraditional gender roles by both women and men, breadwinning responsibilities, and the ability to fulfill them, continue to be particularly salient for married men's well-being," she wrote.

Marisa Frank, a former project accountant turned full-time mom from Medford, Oregon, has witnessed this combination of modern yet manly firsthand. When they were both working, her husband Matt was the very picture of the caring, family-oriented father that has been much-hailed by the media over the past few years. He took turns changing the diapers of their two young boys; he handled the family's morning routine—getting his older son dressed, fed, and dropped off at preschool, where Marisa would pick him up in the afternoons—and he by and large did what he could to keep their lives balanced. "We really did split things," Marisa says appreciatively. But when child-care costs began to outweigh the benefits of having two incomes, Marisa saw a different side to her husband—the side that felt fully responsible for solving the problem.

A few years later, when the stress of maintaining a career and caring for their two sons started to weigh on Marisa, both parents believed the solution lay in stepping up Matt's career and scaling back Marisa's. "It wasn't even something we had to debate—we both knew that I would be happier at home whereas he would be miserable." Together they collaborated to make up for her lost income. Matt landed a job in a different city that offered a 50 percent increase over his previous salary, while Marisa agreed to relocate the family. "I never would have thought before I'd be so open to moving. But once I realized it meant I could leave my job, I was on board," she says.

As she recalls the first time she noticed her husband establishing himself as their breadwinner, Marisa breaks into a stifled laugh. "From the beginning of our marriage anytime it looked like I might start to make more money than him, he would find ways to make sure his paycheck was bigger. And this was way before we even thought about having kids, so I really couldn't see why it should matter so much to him. . . . For some reason, whenever I would get a raise, next thing I know he'd come home telling me he'd gone to his boss and asked for one too." Even more amusing to Marisa, Matt's boss, Steve, was not only almost always receptive to Matt's request, but sympathetic to his reasoning for it as well. "Matt and his boss were pretty good friends and it was a family-owned company, so he would tell him honestly, 'Marisa got a raise, so I need one too.' And that usually worked. I mean, by then it was pretty much time for him to get a pay increase anyway, but I thought it was hilarious that they both thought that was a perfectly valid reason for asking."

Did it ever bother her, I ask, or strike her as offensively chauvinistic? "No. Not really. I actually thought it was cute. I mean, if anything, it made me feel cared for, like I knew I could count on him if times got tough."

Obviously, not every man is going to care whether he's bringing home the bigger portion of the household income, but Matt Frank is one example of what Feldhahn, the Pew Center, Weiss, and many others have documented. Part of most men's identities, especially how they see themselves in relation to their wife and children, is tied up with how well they do at work.

Women tend to categorize work and family as two separate issues; to men they are inextricable. Ask yourself, as a woman, how central what you do for a living is to your idea of who you are. For most of us it is one element of many. You might think of yourself first as a mother, a wife, or a friend. But your first thought probably isn't an unconflicted *I am a lawyer*. Or if it is your first thought, the lawyer part of your identity probably stands alone. You don't think, *I am a mother, therefore I am a lawyer*. You don't think, *I am someone's wife, therefore I teach school*.

When you ask a married man who he is, his first answer may not be his job title (then again, it very well may), but any answer he gives is going to be inextricably tied to his ability to earn. He may not consider his job as a lawyer or a teacher his primary function in life, but odds are he sees it as a vital element in all the other roles he plays. Whereas many mothers report feeling torn and guilty about the hours they spend at work, worrying about the impact it has on their children, fathers typically say the opposite. They feel guilty if they're not working enough. "Work," as one expert put it, "is important for men's lives partly because it is the foundation for everything else."

## Marriage and Masculinity

So the questions for us now are *why* your husband gets so much of his identity and self-esteem from his work and *what* you can do with that knowledge. After studying the behavior of men, and particularly husbands, for years, sociologist Steven Nock of the University of Virginia had some answers.

While working on his award-winning book *Marriage in Men's Lives,* Dr. Nock wanted to uncover what it is about marriage that changes men. Not just what makes them happier, healthier, and wealthier, but what about it makes them *better.* Because as Nock demonstrates, in most of the ways we would typically associate with being an upstanding and productive citizen, marriage does make men better. They become better workers, they take better care of their family members, they become more involved in improving their communities, and they give more of their money away to charitable causes. Through all of these endeavors, men accept more responsibility for the world around them. This happens, Nock explains, because becoming a husband is the key that unlocks the door to masculine maturity. "Marriage is the only way that most males can become men," he contends. "It is through marriage, more than anything else, that they conform to the shared ideals of manhood." And foremost among those ideals is being a provider.

Just by listening to the way we refer to masculinity versus femininity in our common language, we learn that men and women attain maturity through different methods. While boys are told to "be a man" when facing something frightening, few girls (outside of a joke) have ever been admonished to "be a woman." Because their ability to bear children is a clear enough marker, rarely have societies demanded that girls prove themselves worthy of womanhood. Boys, on the other hand, throughout history and within countless cultures, have had to conquer all manner of challenges to earn the right to be called men. The fact that almost all those challenges involve providing materially for others suggests that it may stem from a biological drive in men's natures.

Once upon a time (and even now in some places) a man was required to give a "bride price"—money or goods—to a woman's family to prove he could afford a wife. Among Comanches, after a boy had completed his rite of passage by killing a buffalo, he often had to work for his potential father-in-law until he established he would be able to take care of the man's daughter. And several African tribes still require a boy to hunt, kill, and distribute the meat of an antelope before he can be considered a man. Failure to do so will prohibit him from ever being permitted to marry.

The industrialized world may not have such clear-cut tasks that allow someone who once was a boy to be recognized as a mature man and thus a viable candidate for marriage, but being able to provide for others is still a big part of it. After researching thousands of men over the course of several decades, Nock found that even in today's gender-bending world, marriage and the ability to supply the needs of a family continue to be the clearest markers of masculinity.

"One of the things I developed in that book is that at least for a large number of men it seems that marriage is serving both the emotional and psychological purposes that we expect it to, but it also gives men a claim to being a full-fledged member of the male persuasion—they are truly men," says Nock. "Being a man historically and traditionally, whether it's in this country or elsewhere, has meant providing for the family and being an earner. That was true hundreds of years ago and to some extent it's true now."

To get a full understanding of the masculine ideal, Nock says, you have to ask, "What does it mean to be a man? How do you demonstrate that you are in fact a masculine guy? I know when people first hear it, they think it has to do with being macho, buff, or athletic or that sort of thing. I can see that sounds like masculinity, but when you really get down to it, and try to study what the ideals of masculine identity are, they are conformity to a whole bunch of expectations about what it means to be dependable and what it means to be steadfast and faithful and all those things. And by the way, those are the expectations and requirements that men most encounter when they get married. . . . The fact that a man is a husband carries great significance to others."

It also carries great significance to the man himself, because it is the clearest indicator that he has become independent. A boy looks to others to take care of him. But as a husband and as a father, he assumes the role of taking care of people who depend on him. As one Fortune 500 board chairman said of how his own work ethic developed, "Left to my own devices, I felt no compulsion to strive. [But after marriage] my wife became my focus and the person to whom I owed my best. . . . She was the person to whom I felt accountable, and therefore I tried."

This probably explains why men would work even if their spouses could comfortably support them. They don't work just so they can provide, but so they can legitimately see themselves as providers. While the progress wives have made in the workforce has had many wonderful benefits for both men and women, one of the downsides is that it has left men feeling that they aren't entitled to see themselves that way anymore.

When men feel that their wives don't need them to take care of them financially, it can present a problem for both spouses. As we've seen, feeling that their husbands aren't good providers causes many wives to resent them and with-draw from them both physically and emotionally. For men, the impact is even worse.

Well-known family therapist Michael Gurian notes that "men feel for their careers what most of their male ancestors felt in the hunt and conquest—that [it] is a sacred way of developing inherent worth." Imagine, then, what a man feels when he believes that he isn't doing well in his work. The sense of worthlessness that follows can manifest itself in withdrawing, insecurity, anger, inertia, and depression. This creates a vicious circle. A wife is irritated that her husband isn't doing well enough in his work, and she expresses this feeling in various ways. The husband then feels as though he's letting his family down, sinks deeper into a malaise, and continues to underachieve. Even when a man is providing for his family, he can feel insecure about how well he's doing.

But there is a way around it. Through purposeful interaction with your husband, you can harness and enhance the power of the marriage premium. By affirming his work as significant and his role as provider as important, you can motivate a man who is already doing well to achieve even more. And if he is floundering and doesn't outwardly appear to be a good provider, your interaction with him can help him start to become one.

## The Michelangelo Phenomenon

We all have visions of who we think we should be and might become with enough effort. These characteristics make up our ideal self, and they differ from person to person. For some people, being humorous is an ideal quality—they feel closest to being their best self when they make others laugh.

But someone else might not consider being funny that important. Instead, they see empathy as an ideal characteristic, so they feel at their best when they have opportunities to show compassion. Because an individual's self-esteem corresponds to how closely he or she embodies his or her ideal, those who believe they are moving toward it have a greater sense of well-being. They are happier with themselves and with their relationships; they are also more positive and proactive in pursuing goals. Conversely, people who do not believe they possess the qualities they see as ideal or rarely have opportunities to display them are less productive and tend to be unhappy with themselves and their relationships.

Psychologists have found that spouses have a tremendous power to help each other become either more or less like their ideal selves. We've all heard the phrase "You bring out the best in me." To most people, it represents little more than a bit of romantic hyperbole. But a pattern called the Michelangelo Phenomenon proves that in good relationships the maxim is actually true.

While the name suggests some kind of museum-heist movie or a sequel to the hit novel *The Da Vinci Code,* the Michelangelo Phenomenon actually describes a relationship dynamic that occurs between couples. Art historians have long recounted the legend that Michelangelo's genius lay in the fact that where other sculptors looked at a piece of marble and decided what they wanted to make of it, he looked at the marble and saw what it wanted to be. That is, he was able to see the potential in a hunk of rock and cut away all the extraneous matter until he revealed the ideal form hidden inside. Psychologists use this metaphor to describe the effect one romantic partner has on the other when the partner's perceptions and behaviors help "sculpt" the other into his or her "ideal self."

When a wife says and does things that show her husband she believes that he possesses his ideal qualities, he in turn lives up to her vision and moves closer to embodying them. In effect, her beliefs about him act as self-fulfilling prophecies that sculpt him into his ideal, just as Michelangelo did with marble. The bad news is that her unbelief is equally influential in moving him further away from his best self. As Stephen Drigotas of John Hopkins University put it, "Our romantic partners have considerable influence (affirming or disaffirming) over what we become. . . . Having a partner who behaves in a manner that sculpts one's ideal self is not only good for the relationship, but it is good for one's personal well-being as well."

While the qualities people consider ideal differ depending on their culture, genetics, and family influence, there is, as we have seen, at least one that is universal to men. Most men, especially after they become husbands, believe they should be good providers. Even if your husband doesn't act as if providing is important to him, the research confirms that, deep in his heart, he probably still sees it as an "ideal quality" he ought to have. And if you don't think he has it, he is unlikely to think so too. Even if you do see him as an able provider, if you don't indicate that belief to him, it will have no impact in moving him closer to his ideal. This is crucial because some studies on the Michelangelo Phenomenon not only confirmed its effect, they also found that men are more sensitive to disparities between their spouse's view of them and their ideal self than women are.

When they felt they were failing to provide for their

families Dr. Weiss's subjects often fell into deep holes of in-security, anxiety, and isolation. "Their self-blame," he wrote, "can be bottomless even if the fault was not theirs." Yet be-cause they cared so much about their wives' opinion of them and wanted to protect it, they usually didn't risk it by admit-ting failure. Instead they kept all these feelings to themselves, releasing tension in sometimes harmless, but sometimes destructive, ways. Men who feel that they're not living up to the ideal of taking care of their families can suffer all manner of harmful symptoms, from depression to self-medicating through alcohol, drugs, and food. So the very negative behav-ior that keeps a man from doing well in the workplace could stem from the hit his self-esteem takes from being so far from his ideal. After his study, Weiss concluded that men "need their wives to see them as competent because their wives' view of them is so important to their view of themselves."

What Weiss, Nock, and others have discovered dovetails perfectly with how the chairman of Time Warner's board, Richard Parsons, describes his own transformation from un-derachieving party guy to formidable businessman:

> When I got married, it mattered that my wife think well of me. And it mattered that she have a positive sense not only of who I was, but of what I was doing and how hard I was trying. I couldn't just hang around wasting time anymore because I wanted to have her favor in terms of her assessment of me as a person. So if she came home and said, "What are you doing, goofing around again?" I'd think, "Aw, geez, I'd better shape up because I don't want my wife thinking I'm a goof-off."
>
> I'm certain I would not have followed the career track that I ended up following if I hadn't been married be-

*cause I'm actually more of a passive type B personality than a hard-charging type A. To the extent that I have ambition, it's probably more because I don't want to let her down than I'm trying to prove something to myself, because on my own I don't really operate on that level.*

Wives have an inherent effect on their husbands' growth. That effect may be to stall or even retard progress, or it may be to advance it further, faster, but you are sculpting your husband one way or another. So for his good as well as yours, you might as well sculpt him into his ideal.

The sculpting that takes place during the Michelangelo Phenomenon occurs through three steps. (1) You identify the qualities your husband sees as ideal. (2) You affirm that he has these qualities and behave in a way that allows him to display them. (3) That affirmation results in his taking actions that move him closer to his ideal, and his resulting sense of well-being provides positive reinforcement for continuing his progress. For example, we know that most men see being a good provider as an ideal quality. So if you make appreciative comments about, say, how nice it is in this era of deadbeat dads to know you have a man you can count on, you affirm the part of him that wants to be a provider. If you show your belief in his ability to provide during lean times by saying you know how capable he is and know your situation is only temporary, he will continue to see himself as a provider despite the circumstances and feel positive energy to overcome it. By the same token, if you make jokes or bitter comments about his inability to bring home a decent paycheck, you increase the likelihood that he'll continue underearning.

If you've ever seen the romantic comedy *High Fidelity* starring John Cusack, it provides a good example of this process.

Cusack's character, Rob, is filled with self-loathing and insecurity because he is nowhere near what he sees as the ideal man—someone productive and creative. We know what qualities Rob considers ideal because he idolizes musicians for "bringing something new into the world" and fantasizes about being a writer for *Rolling Stone*. Rob, on the other hand, doesn't create anything, and he certainly isn't productive. He runs a dilapidated used-record store that is causing him to go broke. He clearly wants to carve out a better life for himself, but he has been trapped in extended adolescence so long that he doesn't know how to begin. And his unhappiness with himself makes him negative, selfish, and obsessive.

Rob's girlfriend, Laura, can see that many of the problems in their relationship stem from Rob's inability to grow into the man he wants to be. He scorns his two underachieving employees, whom he calls "the musical moron twins," for displaying the same characteristics he dislikes in himself—they don't have any plans for the future and their knowledge of obscure music is taking them nowhere. He makes snide comments about Laura's rising salary, indicating that her professional growth is a sore spot for him. Though it's a painful process that almost ends their relationship, Laura helps Rob see that he too is capable of growth. She demonstrates her belief that he possesses his ideal qualities by encouraging him to start a record label, a venture that requires both creativity and productivity. When Rob decides to give it a go, she again affirms her belief by arranging a promotional event at a club so he can kick off his new career officially. At the end of the movie, we see Rob wrap his arms around Laura and gaze at the crowd at his first record-release party, finally looking satisfied and happy with his life.

As the narrative above illustrates, the Michelangelo Phenomenon happens not just by encouraging words, but also through creating opportunities for your husband to display his ideal qualities. If he is someone like my husband who sees a good sense of humor as ideal, then you would not only laugh at his jokes, you would create openings at parties for him to tell a funny story. With the provider ideal, you embrace opportunities for him to, well, provide. This might mean supporting (within reason) his long work schedules or his furthering of his education. It might mean returning to your dating roles when you go out to dinner, allowing him to chivalrously pick up the check. There are infinite possibilities for how this might play out in your household. The Michelangelo Phenomenon isn't a strict formula; it only requires you to take advantage of opportunities to affirm your husband as provider verbally and with your actions when these opportunities present themselves.

When I had asked Dr. Nock about his personal experience with the ability of wives to affirm their husbands as providers, he was quick to confirm that his own wife had done just that for him. "What she did," he said, "was to make me feel that my job was very, very important not only to me, but also to her." Specifically, she was willing to relocate for his work. Says Nock, "We both got out of grad school at the same time and we both got our careers going at the same time. And we ended up in separate cities and wanted to be together. So the question was, 'Do I move to her place or does she move to mine?'" She moved to his, which meant, he recalls, "taking a less prestigious position—that's what she was giving up." He admitted that though the disparity was never intentional, over the years he had not done an equal amount to promote her professional goals: "My wife has made more personal sacrifices in the name of my career. . . . But I have made personal concessions for her especially as it pertains to our family and her relations and so forth. I think what my wife did for me, maybe it's a traditional pattern . . . but I've also found that there's some power in the traditional patterns as long as they're not experienced as being unfair."

Would Steven Nock have become a nationally recognized scholar, whose work has been analyzed and discussed by nearly every major newspaper in the country, had his wife not made it known that she considered his work important and had her actions not suggested that she expected him to do well? Perhaps, but Nock certainly seemed to feel that her support played a major part in it.

It's important to note that the Michelangelo Phenomenon isn't a selfish, manipulative process—it is something that strengthens relationships and makes both partners happier with the other. While behaving in a way that moves your husband toward the masculine ideal of being a good provider may benefit you and your family financially, it will benefit him psychologically. Though it is a powerful tool, the Michelangelo Phenomenon also isn't a magic trick that will help you shape your husband into any form you wish him to take. If you think being frugal is an ideal quality but he sees generosity as his ideal, then affirming him as a thrifty person isn't suddenly going to make him start counting every penny. Even worse, when one partner affirms qualities that aren't a part of the other's ideal self, it can actually damage the relationship as it moves them further from the person they want to be. It may sound trite, but it doesn't go too far to say women can make or break their men. When wives reflect back to their husbands' closely held beliefs about who they want to be, their wives help them move closer to that ideal.

The very fact that you are reading this book indicates that

you take your husband's work seriously. So all of the principles you are about to learn from the wives in the following chapters contribute to the Michelangelo Phenomenon. You will not only see results from each lesson you apply in the immediate sense, you will also see secondary results, because they all demonstrate your belief in your man in his role as provider.

## TAKEAWAY FACTS TO ENCOURAGE AND CHALLENGE YOU

1. In addition to the anecdotal evidence you will find in this book, there is sound and wide-ranging statistical evidence that you can have a profound effect on your husband's income. It may not be the equivalent of a second full-time job (then again it may), but you can feel confident that a part of his earnings is due to you!

2. For all the social changes we have seen in the last thirty years, men still see providing for their family as a vital part of their identity. It is one of the most important factors in allowing them to feel good about themselves as men. Research in both sociology and psychology shows that men experience greater life satisfaction when they believe themselves to be good providers.

3. When you affirm in your husband the masculine ideal of being a provider through your words and actions, he will move closer to becoming one. No one else has as much ability to shape your husband into his best self as you.

# How Taking a Step Back Can Move Your Husband Closer to the Top and You Closer to Home

Remember back in high school, when we all (even if we knew it was just an exercise that would have no bearing on our future) had to visit the guidance counselor to discuss what career we should pursue after graduation? We took tests that measured our aptitude and considered recommendations based on the results. The idea wasn't necessarily to set us on a path for life but to get us to square one—identifying a job that might eventually serve as a launching pad to a long-term profession.

My husband was seven years out of college, but if I ever hoped for him to have a career that he could feel ambitious in, that was where we had to return—square one. And that may be where you are right now. Your husband doesn't yet have a vision for success. He may be working in a job that to him is just a job and as a result doesn't have many specific goals. As we've seen, this situation is particularly common among men in their twenties and early thirties.

Even if your spouse is in a field that suits him, doing a job he enjoys, that doesn't mean he's going to stay there. If he remains in the same company, he may find he needs to move into another department to get on the executive track or that he's better at marketing than sales. Or he may suddenly realize that the area he's working in is becoming obsolete in today's global economy, and he either has to adapt or risk being downsized.

The problem for wives is that confronting the fact that

their husbands might need to return to square one can be a scary thing. Even when we intellectually know that you sometimes have to break a bone to reset it properly, the specter of experience lost or education down the drain looks too painful to contemplate. This was especially true in my case, because when Brian did decide what he wanted to start over in, it was a business in which age plays a crucial role. Granted, in that respect women in broadcasting have it much worse than men, but I still worried that he was entering an already hypercompetitive field at a disadvantage.

Even though I believed it was the right move for him, I had to force myself to let go of "if only" thinking. *If only Brian had realized right out of college that he should go into television journalism. Where would he be now if he had started seven years ago?* It was pointless and unproductive, and it stemmed from my belief that he was behind everyone else because he didn't do it the "right" way (the right way meaning starting in a field at twenty-four and sticking with it until retirement).

But after closing my eyes and taking the plunge, I discovered two things:

(1) Everybody else isn't following as straight a career path as we tend to think. This notion that the "right" way to approach work is to pick a profession, get a job with a good company, and slowly rise through the ranks is outdated. These days one of the biggest keys to success is flexibility. Before becoming host of the highly-rated MSNBC debate show *Hardball,* Chris Matthews transitioned through multiple fields. All involved his first love, politics, but building a lucrative career out of that love took several stops and restarts.

During his first few years in Washington, Matthews worked as a Capitol Hill staffer before campaigning to become a congressman himself. He lost. He then, according to his wife Kathleen, "went from being a White House speech-writer [for President Carter] to being unemployed for a short period of time, because he couldn't really figure out what he wanted to do, to working for the Democratic Campaign Committee to working for [Speaker of the House] Tip O'Neill. And then he worked for a consulting firm for less than a year, because he realized very quickly that he didn't like it. Finally he took a 200 percent cut in his salary to work as a newspaper columnist for the *San Francisco Examiner*."

On paper (or at least on pay stubs) it might have looked as though Matthews was moving backward rather than forward. But through each of these steps, Matthews and Kathleen discovered where his gifts lay and how to make the most of them. After honing his talent for analyzing politicians and policies as a columnist for two years, Matthews was promoted to Washington, D.C., bureau chief. It was at this time, says his wife, that he discovered how well his debate skills translated to another medium: "After doing a lot of speeches and a lot of TV appearances as a commentator, he realized he wanted to go into television full-time. I had some doubts, but I knew that if he really wanted to do it, he could do it. So he took a job with an unknown, untested cable network called America's Talking, which later became MSNBC."

Though she acknowledges that going through so many transitions with Matthews was sort of like "leaping off cliffs," she says that for her the choice was still a "no-brainer": "I tend to be very averse to risk for myself but not for him. . . . If anything, I was an enabler for his risk taking. But it was a good kind of enabling—not the kind you have to go to therapy for." Kathleen says she encouraged Matthews to pursue different avenues to use his talent because "I always knew that if Chris could find the right place to use his passion for politics and passion for the country, it would be something he would love and he would be tremendously successful."

It was partly because of his wife's insistence that he not get mired down in a job that didn't really fit him that Matthews finally found himself doing "exactly what he probably in high school believed he should be doing but just couldn't have defined it then." The bonus of course is that not only does Matthews now love his work, he is one of the best-compensated and most recognizable figures in his field.

Like Matthews, the majority of the successful men I researched made significant turns in direction at some point in their careers. Even after they were clear on their goals and had formulated a plan, many later found that the plan had to be restructured if they were to get where they wanted to go. Fortunately for them, they didn't see them as setbacks because they had wives who understood the value of those turns.

(2) All that said, people constantly make changes in their careers that don't necessarily move them forward. Today the average person changes jobs seven to ten times over the course of his or her life. Younger workers, between the ages of eighteen and thirty-eight, burn through three of those switches in the first five years. So clearly not everyone who switches gears ends up moving faster toward the top.

The difference for Matthews and those like him is that their changes were made in service to their strengths. Whether it was as a political aide, a columnist, or a talk-show host, Matthews was constantly trying to find the position that would best utilize his greatest skills.

At this point you might be thinking that taking risks to serve his strengths worked out for Matthews because he was ambitious from the outset. If your husband hasn't ever shown any enthusiasm for his work, you might doubt that he ever will. But even the most dedicated slackers can find inner drive when they hit on an area that utilizes their natural gifts.

When Laura Parsons first met her husband Richard, nothing about him indicated that he would eventually rise to become CEO of Time Warner and one of the most respected businessmen of his time. Unlike so many corporate leaders, Parsons didn't have an Ivy League background to help launch his career, and he certainly didn't have their connections. Known for being a bit of a partyer, he was, by his own recollection, "a miserable student" during his high school years.

This is usually the point in an inspirational story where the author reveals that young Parsons turned himself around after going away to school and resolved to put in long, hard hours to reach the top. But none of this was true in Parsons's case. Or at least not yet. In fact, his tendency to let good times take precedence over serious study didn't change even after a basketball scholarship paved his way to the University of Hawaii. Once there, the distractions of girls and an active fraternity scene took a toll on his grade-point average. He left school six credits short of a degree in history.

At a crossroads and unsure what to do with himself, the young woman he was dating at the time had a radical idea. "You know," said Laura, "you should think about being a lawyer." Most people would have reacted to her suggestion with more than a little skepticism, considering that Parsons's track record up to that point didn't exactly scream "future law school valedictorian," but Laura knew that her boyfriend wouldn't have any real aspirations until he found something that matched his aptitudes. "You like to argue so much," she said, "you ought to get paid for it." He decided to take the law school entrance exams.

Her advice turned out to be just the thing Parsons needed. He had always been intelligent, but he'd never found a course of study that challenged him enough to keep him engaged. Once he'd stumbled on a subject that fit his strengths, Parsons displayed a fierce work ethic, and astounding results quickly followed. He graduated first in his class from law school and received the highest score in the state of New York on his bar exam. This set the stage for a widely varied career that has included serving as a White House aide to President Gerald Ford, making partner at a prestigious law firm, and taking the helm of what was at the time the largest media conglomerate in the world.

Looking back on it all, he credits Laura for much of his success, saying it was she who taught him "how to get serious—about my career, my life, and the goals I should set for myself." The study of the law, he says, "gave me the discipline I was looking for, a discipline I embraced myself instead of one my parents and teachers had to struggle to impose." Incidentally, it was also Laura who, when the corporate world came knocking, prodded her husband to apply his strengths in a new direction by becoming a leader himself rather than remaining legal counsel for leaders.

No matter how much people resolve to tackle their career with renewed determination, they are going to have a difficult time doing so unless their work matches their talents. When they do match, it is almost as if resolutions become irrelevant—they reach goals and see improvement so rapidly, they have ample incentive to keep pushing forward. So as frightening as it can feel in the present, as long as it is made in service to his strengths, returning to square one (or square two, three, or four) could end up being a giant leap forward for your husband.

## Understanding Strengths

According to a Gallup poll, only 20 percent of today's labor force believe their jobs utilize their best assets. Only 20 percent. That means 80 percent of workers are doing a job they don't really believe they are suited for. Is it any wonder then that most people tend toward a clock-in, clock-out attitude when it comes to their careers? Even if they are conscientious employees who are looking to advance, odds are the hours and effort they put into doing so feel like a slog. This goes a long way to explaining why so few people move ahead rapidly, showing the kind of superproductivity that makes the world (and employers) sit up and take notice. The difference isn't usually one of talent—plenty of talented people linger in the middle of the pack—and it isn't even necessarily one of discipline. It is a question of fit. Does your husband's job fit his strengths? Or does his approach to his job fit his strengths?

While doing research for his book *Now, Discover Your Strengths*, Gallup Organization senior vice president Marcus Buckingham discovered that the highest achievers are in positions where they are able to utilize their strengths every day. Using an extensive, long-term study of 2 million professionals classified as "excellent performers," he found that the general public's approach to achievement is completely backward. Most people focus on their areas of weakness, attending training sessions and pinpointing "opportunities for growth" during their annual reviews. By filling in those gaps and becoming fairly competent at everything, they reason, they will be more likely to move ahead. In reality this approach keeps people from excelling in any one area while sentencing them to mediocrity in most.

The biggest problem with most people's thinking when it comes to strengths and weaknesses is that we were all taught growing up that with enough effort and desire, anyone can become good at anything. Unfortunately, experts in a variety of fields have found that this is false. Said one researcher, "Neuroscience tells us a person's talent does not change significantly over time, and leaders will improve the most in their areas of greatest talent." And really, when you consider the idea with a bit of common sense, it isn't all that surprising. Your husband might become *better* at a particular skill, but unless that ability is in some sense natural, he will never become great. He can't help it—his brain won't have it any other way.

In recent years neuroscientists have made great strides in determining where human talent comes from. What they have discovered is that between the nerve cells in our brains that process information are billions of threads that carry data from one cell to another. These are called axons, which meet at synapses, and as our brains develop into adulthood, the less-used synaptic connections wither away, meaning some nerve cells stop communicating with one another or don't communicate very well. Neurologists speculate that a combination of genetics and early-childhood experiences determines which threads we will lose, but that the lack of communication between nerve cells creates our weak areas. For example, if your husband has trouble coordinating large projects, it's probably because his synaptic connections are weak when it comes to organization. On the positive side, the synaptic connections that our environment and DNA compel us to use often grow stronger, forming our strengths. What this means is that your husband's talents are, for the most part, fixed, and his greatest potential for excellence lies in the areas where he has the strongest synaptic connections. A person has to exercise that connection to capitalize on it, but the building material of the skill is already encased in his head.

While on the surface this news can come off a little depressing (those shy husbands aren't ever going to become the life of the party), it is also liberating. Neither you nor he has to waste time watching him strain to perfect skills that leave him feeling frustrated and discouraged. Even better, he can redirect his energy into areas he already has a knack for and relish the experience of seeing results very quickly.

If you've ever known someone who you thought of as lazy or shiftless who suddenly became wildly motivated after starting a new career, it is probably because he or she finally found an area of expertise that made use of their natural talents. Before, they were trying to force themselves to exhibit abilities or pursue work that didn't make use of their strongest synaptic connections. This doesn't mean that diligence doesn't play a role in goal achievement, or that it isn't sometimes necessary to overcome a difficult challenge. But it does mean that no matter how much you think your husband needs to excel at a certain skill, if it isn't an area where he has strong synaptic connections, there isn't much chance he's going to. Better to reorganize his career priorities around the strengths he does have than make him ineffective (and probably miserable) by pestering him to grow ones he doesn't have.

Now, don't take this to mean that your husband should never bother with anything he isn't immediately good at—obviously basic aptitude in certain areas is necessary for getting along in life. Just think of it in terms of investment versus return: if he focuses the majority of his energy on his weaknesses, he will be wasting valuable time and effort that could be better spent elsewhere. As we grow, we literally become wired to be gifted at different things, and when your spouse ignores the areas he is gifted at to obsess over a skill that he isn't gifted at, he cheats his real gifts. Successful people don't cheat their gifts.

## Identifying Strengths

The first step in helping your husband find his square one (or square two or three, depending on where he is and how big of a change he needs to make) is identifying his strengths. There are countless career-coaching companies that offer tests to determine strengths and just as many Web resources that offer the same (the Gallup organization has a good one at Strengthsfinder.com). While strengths testing can be fun, however, it isn't essential. Chances are you know your husband well enough to know some of his strengths already, and isolating more is simply a matter of paying attention.

Laura, the future Mrs. Parsons, didn't need expensive analysis to know that her boyfriend was a persuasive linear thinker, she only had to listen to how well he constructed arguments around a point. Kathleen Matthews didn't need a test to tell her that her husband's ability to find a fresh spin on provoking political issues would make for riveting television. If there are certain tasks your husband always performs well, like identifying patterns or rallying people toward a course of action, those are undoubtedly two of his strengths. But not all his strengths will be immediately apparent. There are easy methods you can use to identify the less obvious ones.

First, look for areas of yearning. Often our desire to pursue a particular dream is born out of our unconscious awareness of our strengths. Depending on the dream, your husband may not want to pursue it in its present form, but it can provide helpful clues about the qualities that led to it.

Growing up, my husband always wanted to be an actor. For a variety of reasons, he never pursued that dream, and by the time he was a married thirty-something man, it wouldn't have been the most practical course of action to pack our bags and head for Hollywood. Maybe it would have been the right decision for a braver, more free-spirited couple, but for us another dream—starting a family and being able to provide for it—was more important. But Brian's childhood ambition did help us isolate his grown-up strengths and decide how he might use them in a new career. Being a good broadcaster also involves capturing and holding an audience's attention. Interviewing guests on a morning show requires the ability to play off other people to entertain viewers. Anchoring, interviewing, and presenting the weather aren't acting in the purest sense, but they draw on a lot of the same skills.

Still, sometimes, for a variety of reasons, such as a wrongheaded notion of how glamorous a certain job might be, yearnings can be misleading. Your husband may long to sing on Broadway, but if he doesn't have the pipes to back it up, then you can probably ignore that yearning—it isn't one of his strengths (though addressing crowds might be). So it is important to cross-reference yearnings with a second investigational tool: skills that he learns easily.

If your accountant husband is asked to attend a corporate-communications seminar and suddenly finds that he is the best in his class and uses by instinct most of the techniques the instructor suggests, he may need to find a way to combine his accounting skills and his communication skills to get the most out of his career—both the most compensation and the most enjoyment. He might start offering his own training sessions to the accounting department, or he could look for ways to play the lead role in making sure different sections in his department understand one another and have clarity on a project. As Buckingham discovered during his research, "whether the skill is selling, presenting, architectural drafting, giving developmental feedback to an employee, preparing legal briefs, writing business plans ... if you learn it rapidly, you should look deeper. You will be able to identify the talent or talents that made it possible."

A third approach to identifying strengths is noting the tasks that bring your husband the most satisfaction. Because our strengths fire from the most active parts of our brain, exercising them produces a sense of elation—basically, using them feels good. People who are especially coordinated or rhythmically gifted possess synaptic connections that someone like me, who has a hard time mastering a simple box step, doesn't. And they feel a rush when they exercise them.

If spending hours solving challenging logic puzzles leaves your husband feeling exhilarated rather than frustrated, he needs to exploit this facility for problem-solving on the job. Even if his hobby doesn't look like something that could be considered a strength, it might be hiding an ability that could be applied to his work.

As clinical director of the Family Therapy Institute of Santa Barbara, psychologist Don MacMannis is constantly able to exercise his gift for understanding and working with children, so he has never questioned whether he is in the right field. But it took his wife's vision to help him see how another of his strengths might enable him to help kids on a wider scale. After watching her husband dabble in his music room on the weekends, Debra MacMannis realized that he should try his hand at writing children's songs. "You're like a kid. You love kids. That's what you're supposed to do," she told him.

He took her advice, and PBS soon hired him as music director and songwriter for their hit children's program *Jay Jay the Jet Plane.* Adults without young kids may not recognize Jay Jay's name, but ask any parent of a three- to five-year-old and they will tell you that in toddler world, the cartoon about the little blue airplane is more popular than *American Idol.* Tiny fans of the show loved McMannis's melodies, and their moms and dads loved his educational lyrics. Their reaction was so encouraging, it led him to record two award-winning children's CDs filled with songs designed to teach kids important social and emotional skills. Dr. MacMannis's record sales and work for PBS increased his income, but more important, they increased his career satisfaction. He is now able to have a positive impact on kids who will never come to his office. And it wouldn't have happened had his wife Debra not recognized the potential in her husband's hobby.

You may not want your husband to take up professional gambling just because he's a good poker player, but his skill at the card table could be evidence that he's a tough negotiator, something that's a major asset in any number of business situations. Hobbies like model-building require focus and precision, just as many technical and engineering positions do.

When it comes to recreational activities, we typically choose to spend the most time at those we enjoy. And we enjoy them because they come easily to us, meaning they make use of our strengths. Whatever hobby your husband indulges in, note the strengths it draws on and analyze whether he's using that strength at the office.

One other technique came up often during my research

on the wives of successful men. Many said that their husband's strengths were simply common knowledge to anyone who knew him. When the people who have worked for him or had business dealings with him discuss Richard Parsons, the same descriptions tend to pop up again and again. Adjectives like "persuasive" and "diplomatic" appear in almost every newspaper or magazine profile of him. "People do things for Dick because he persuaded them to, not because he ordered them to," said Leo Hindery, former CEO of a sports group owned by Time Warner. Richard J. Bressler, former chief financial officer of Viacom, commented, "What you have to understand about Dick is that he's the consummate diplomat. . . . He was always able to bring people together as a way to harmonize the company." And Rudy Giuliani told the *New York Times* Parsons "really knows how to bring people together to find a common ground." So I would add another criterion for identifying a strength: When everyone around your husband seems to notice a particular talent of his and comments on it, that's probably a good time to stop and consider whether he is using it to its full potential.

It's also worth noting that strengths aren't hierarchical. Just because your husband's strengths differ from someone else's, that doesn't mean he is less likely to do well at work. Parsons used strengths like diplomacy and persuasion to carve out a reputation for being able to come into volatile corporate environments, calm everyone down, and smooth out bad feelings so that employees could refocus on their goals. He doesn't try to mimic the strengths of other CEOs, as the *Financial Times* pointed out when they noted that unlike so many of today's top business leaders, Parsons "does not seek to be a visionary or technological innovator." Instead he leads from areas where he has those strong synaptic connections.

By the same token Parsons's approach wouldn't work for every CEO, let alone every businessperson. Other exceptional executives have been described in terms exactly the opposite of Parsons's. Les Moonves, president and CEO of CBS, is routinely described as divisive and hypercompetitive, with an explosive temper. Yet he too is extremely effective in his role, legendary for his ability to draw a sense of loyalty from his staff. If Parsons had tried to behave like a confrontational, tough-as-nails type because it worked for someone else, he probably wouldn't have risen to the position he's in. The same goes for someone like Moonves, who wouldn't have gotten far with Parsons's more cooperative style because it isn't natural to him. So avoid the temptation to compare your husband's strengths with other men's. Whatever they are, if he is in a position to use them to their fullest, he is in a position to succeed.

## Applying Strengths

Even though your husband is aware of his strengths, he may not appreciate their value. Most people err on the side of underestimating rather than overestimating the usefulness of their talents. And they often don't recognize opportunities to apply them until someone, be it a professional career coach, a mentor, or a boss, helps them see how these talents translate to their job responsibilities. In fact, people are so in need of guidance in this area that companies often hire industrial psychologists to run tests on their staff and shadow them during office hours to get a feel for how they might maximize their roles. You, however, are already familiar with your husband's strong points in a way that no consultant can be, so you are in a unique position to be his eyes when he suffers from this kind of myopia.

When I first met my husband Brian, I couldn't help being impressed by the incredible way he had with people. Always having been rather stiff socially myself, I was amazed by his ability to charm large groups of strangers within a matter of seconds. I even told him once that I felt that I was dating the prom king, so often did crowds gather around him. I also noticed he was a phenomenal public speaker, able to adapt his message to his audience and come up with situation-appropriate jokes off-the-cuff. Once we got serious and I openly admitted my appreciation, he was surprised. Because people are always talkative and at ease around him, he just assumed they were that way all the time. He had almost no recognition that bringing out a comfortable feeling of camaraderie in people was a rare ability that he was lucky to possess.

Have you ever marveled at your husband's ability to patiently sit with your child and explain some confusing piece of math homework in such a simple way that the child finally understands it? Is your spouse the one who gets his softball team charged up before the games on Saturday afternoons? Is he the guy whom every neighbor loves to hang around the yard chatting with? Does he enjoy tackling large home projects himself rather than hiring someone to do it? All of these are valuable qualities that should be giving him a leg up at the office.

How often does a company roll out some new policy that isn't as effective as it should be because employees don't understand how to adhere to it? All the employees think they're doing the same thing, but in reality, important customer issues are getting overlooked because departments are working at cross-purposes. The man who is good at explaining steps in an unfamiliar process and why each matters is a man who can do a lot for a business's bottom line. How about the guy who rallies his softball team for the win? If he takes charge of a sales team, he can inspire them to go for the gold just as much as his softball buddies. The popular neighbor is probably going to be just as likable when meeting potential clients, and the home fix-it man's gift for sustaining focus until he solves complicated problems could be used to construct new protocols for safety measures. All of these are contributions that are frequently recognized (and rewarded) in the labor force. Just as a career coach would, you only need to be on the lookout for opportunities and work together to develop an incremental, practical plan for exploiting them. Discuss what's going on at his office and how he might contribute his particular talents. Brainstorm and be creative. Even if he is the boss, there are plenty of situations where he can use his strengths to get more out of his employees.

The final key to applying strengths is allowing and encouraging your husband to adapt them to ever-expanding opportunities. Using strengths is addictive, and as his successes mount up, new avenues for using them are likely to come his way—usually the kind of avenues that carry with them corresponding levels of risk and potential profit. This is where the flexibility factor again comes in. If he avoids the risk, he avoids the profit as well.

By the time Chris Matthews decided to pursue a job in television, he had already established himself in the newspaper business. He could have comfortably remained in print, possibly moving on to a national newsmagazine like *Time* or *Newsweek*. Instead, with Kathleen's backing, he took his skills in a new direction. It took some time ("When he first went on the air it was like a tree falls in the forest and nobody's listening," says Kathleen) but eventually his willingness to try his abilities in a different game paid off.

Even after her husband established himself as a successful

attorney, Laura Parsons continued to urge him to accept challenges to use his strengths in fresh ways. When one of his clients who was on the board of directors at a bank in serious financial trouble decided Richard Parsons was just the person to come in and turn the situation around, Laura encouraged him to go for it.

To his critics, there was no logical reason for Parsons to have been offered the job of chief operating officer at the Dime Bank. He had no background in banking or even in finance, having spent his entire professional life in law. But if there was little apparent cause for the Dime (as New Yorkers know it) to offer him the position, there was even less for Parsons to accept it. He already had a flourishing career and no need to leave the secure path he was on. So why did he risk it? As explanation Parsons says simply, "My wife talked me into it."

Many women would have advised their husbands to stay as far as they could from a situation as dire as the Dime's, and it is doubtful that Laura Parsons would have encouraged her husband to take such a leap—a leap that could have turned out horribly if the Dime had continued its collapse—if she didn't see in him the qualities necessary to turn the bank around. She was right. By drawing on his diplomatic skills, his ability to appease unhappy regulators, and his willingness to enact tough measures, Parsons immediately began to show results. These results eventually led another board of directors to offer him a new challenge, the top seat at Time Warner.

## Preparing for Square One

By nature we are nesters, so striking out on some course of action, no matter what heights it might lead to when the end is unknown and the present is so cozily familiar, is a distasteful prospect to most of us. The majority of wives aren't going to encourage their husbands to select a path of pulling up stakes to move somewhere new or trying a different occupation unless some adversity like job loss or a family crisis forces that choice.

As psychologist Susan Pinker laid out in her book *The Sexual Paradox,* males' greater levels of testosterone gives them "a heightened appetite for competition and risk." Females, on the other hand, boast greater levels of oxytocin, a hormone that leads us to prioritize social networks and caretaking. So now we return to those of you whose husbands really will need to hit the restart button on their careers and head off on a new course. Women are in many ways genetically programmed to give security a higher priority than success.

Unfortunately, risk-management-wise, these are the worst circumstances in which to make a change. Waiting for a crisis means the timing is no longer under your control, and it gives you less room to take action based on what you've learned about your husband's strengths. If he needs to further his education, you won't have time to create a plan that allows him to take classes while still bringing home a paycheck, or to save so that he can return to school full-time. He may scramble to accept any job offer that comes his way, because he didn't have a chance to network his way into the best openings. Basically it reduces you to being reactive instead of proactive.

*Yes, well, we aren't facing any crises and everything's just fine here, thank you very much,* some of you may be thinking. *I suppose my husband doesn't really get to use his strengths at work. And it does kind of seem like he hates his job, but that's life, isn't it? Not everybody gets to like his job. Better that he do*

*okay at something he doesn't like than go down some road*
*where he might not make any money at all.*

If your husband is one of the many people who wish they
were working in a different field or for a different company,
it's understandable that you would feel this way. But based
on the experiences of the wives of many successful men, you
should be careful not to dismiss the possibility of change out
of hand. Not only because you might miss out on the financial rewards that occur when people do what they are best at,
but because you might also miss out on the experience of
being married to a more satisfied, confident man and, thus,
enjoying a more satisfying, happier marriage.

One man I know missed out on two crucial opportunities
to build the kind of career that could have brought him immense satisfaction and could have brought his family a much
higher household income. Once because his wife refused to
move to a new city, and once because she pooh-poohed his
idea of moving from the technical department of his company into training and development (he had been called on
to teach several employee classes at the last minute and discovered he had a knack for it).

How many great careers or public contributions have been
sidelined by a spouse unwilling to gamble a comfortable present on a promising future? How many wives (and husbands,
for that matter) shut the door on opportunity because it
lacked a guaranteed outcome? This is fine if both spouses
agree that they are more interested in security than great
achievements, but if helping your husband become his professional best is the goal, some risk is likely to be involved.
In the majority of the cases in this book, a wife's willingness
to support a calculated gamble in her husband's career paid
off massively. You may have very good reasons for deciding

that a change in your husband's job or location isn't a good choice for your family right now, but make sure you are basing that decision on solid risk assessment and not just fear of the unknown.

The future Laura Parsons didn't risk much when she suggested that her unfocused fiancé consider law school. But she took a big gamble encouraging her lawyer husband to leave his firm and strike out in a new direction. Kathleen Matthews risked financial security when she cheered her husband on as he abandoned a lucrative consulting job for a poorly paid newspaper job, then again when she supported his decision to leave a well-known newspaper for an unknown cable station. But neither took as big a risk as a woman who helped her husband change the face of the retail business and made himself and several of his family members multibillionaires in the process.

Like Richard Parsons, Jeff Bezos was doing very well in his field before he decided to embark on a new adventure. Working in the research department of a Manhattan investment firm, Bezos made a high-six-figure salary. So it had to be at least a bit of a shock for his wife MacKenzie when he decided he wanted them both to quit their jobs (she worked for the same company in a different department), take everything they owned, and move to Seattle to start a website selling books at a time when almost nobody was using the Internet as a retail outlet.

Though their decision has often been characterized as an impulsive lark by business magazines, the Bezoses did plenty of risk analysis before embarking down this unknown road. While researching the Internet for his company's clients in 1994, Bezos stumbled onto the figure that the Internet was growing at a rate of more than 2000 percent per year. At first he thought that figure couldn't be correct, that somewhere someone had made a calculating error. But after further research determined it was accurate, he saw the writing on the wall and started trying to come up with an idea for a company that could capitalize on this underutilized new technology.

He assembled a list of the country's top twenty mail-order catalogues and considered which product would be most convenient for people to purchase online. Soon, he found more than room in a market, he found an almost complete hole. Other than the short children's book order forms kids got at school, there were few options for buying books outside of traditional stores.

But a book business meant moving somewhere he and his wife would have easy access to large warehouse stores of the kind Barnes & Noble and Borders maintained. The best place in the country for that was Seattle. So MacKenzie agreed to head west, driving the 1988 Chevy Blazer that was a gift from Bezos's parents, while he worked on a business plan in the passenger seat.

When they arrived, they settled in a small suburban house and went to work. MacKenzie taught herself an off-the-shelf bookkeeping program and worked as their accounting and research department. They hired a database programmer and a Web programmer, paying their salaries out of their pockets. And in 1995 they launched the site from a garage fitted with desks they had made out of doors to cut costs. They named it Amazon.com after the mighty South American river. And from the day it went online, it was clear it was going to be a huge hit. Amazon.com not only changed the face of the retail business, however, it changed the way MacKenzie Bezos spent her days. After working first as a research assistant at a hedge fund, then as Amazon's accountant, she was finally able to leave the nine-to-five lifestyle altogether and pursue her dream of writing novels.

Had MacKenzie Bezos insisted that such a risk was unnecessary given how well Bezos was doing, he might have scrapped the idea entirely. Instead, Bezos says, "it was easy because my wife was supportive." Though it took faith for her to agree on leaving both their jobs and the life they had known in New York, and spending their savings, it wasn't necessarily blind faith. MacKenzie knew her husband's strengths, knew that identifying market trends was what had made him successful in his previous career and that he was probably right in believing that he had stumbled on a doozy. She knew him to be a visionary yet analytical person and she knew that he would do all the necessary research before heading off. And she knew that she would offer whatever assistance she could to make his dream a reality.

The outcome of a risk is by definition not guaranteed, but you can take certain steps to ensure the odds are in your favor. Do your homework, be as prepared as possible before making a major change, don't leave the outcome completely up to chance, and weigh what you will be giving up if you don't take a chance as much as what you will giving up if you do.

## Do Your Homework

Knowing what you're getting yourselves into before making any major change can alleviate a lot of the fear of risk. If you together decide that your husband needs to be in a different field or at the very least a different job, he shouldn't quit without having a plan about where he is going.

The Bezoses didn't just dream up the idea of the e-bookstore and charge off. They took the time to investigate how viable his idea was. He went to the American Booksellers Association's convention, even attending their introductory course in bookselling. He talked to merchants already in the industry, finding out what it would take to make a business like that work on the Internet. And together they pinpointed the best location in the United States for launching.

Even if you're not starting a business, if your husband is entertaining the idea of a job or career change, assemble as much information as you can about what it will take to make that change successful. Will he need further education? Are there multiple options for the direction he might choose? If so, which of those options best fits your family needs at this time? Does he know people who might be able to give him an inside track at another company? Do you know people who might be able to give him an inside track? He has probably already done a lot of this type of thinking and researching himself. But if you do it along with him, you will reap two benefits:

(1) It will make you a better career counselor because you will have the information necessary to offer input based on the probability of success rather than input arising out of worry, like having to make new friends in a new place. You will be able to act on facts, not fear, and in that you will truly be his partner and career coach, not a shivering flower he is duty-bound not to upset.

(2) It will make the process a lot more fun. When you take part in preparing your husband's next move, it becomes an adventure you are in together. It's the two of you against the world, so when the time comes to finally act, you will have a personal stake in it, and thus the enthusiasm that comes from being a vital part of the process.

## CONSIDER THE COSTS

Deal realistically with what failure could look like and what it will mean to your family if he does fail. But deal *realistically*, not *pessimistically*. Will you really be out on the street if it doesn't work out, or will he just have to take another job doing what he was doing before? Will he have to take a short-term pay cut? Will cutting back really be that unbearable if you know what your smaller budget is in service to? Will you have to relocate temporarily or permanently? Will it really be so bad if your family has to schedule time and take plane trips to come visit you? (For some people, that one could even be looked at as a plus!)

In considering these costs, it is also vital to weigh them against the potential results. If you do have to move or make do with less money for a while, what will those sacrifices mean in the long run? MacKenzie Bezos temporarily sacrificed both a familiar location and financial security, and her husband went from doing well to becoming one of the richest men in the world.

We know people are more likely to advance further and faster in jobs that play to their strengths. So would that mean he has the potential to earn far more in the future than he would if stayed on his current path? What is the upside emotionally? Would he be happier, less stressed, more loving? Would that make you happier, less stressed, and more loving? How much would that affect him as a husband and as a father? How much happier might your marriage be? These concerns are every bit as legitimate as concerns over an unknown future. Count the cost both ways.

True to his strength of having a unique way of seeing the world, Jeff Bezos had a unique way of counting the cost—he called it the "regret-minimization framework." He said that he pictured himself at eighty and knew he would regret not following up on his idea for this amazing new technology more than he would regret trying and failing and missing out on a few six-figure Christmas bonuses. "In fact," he said, "I'd have been proud of myself for having taken that risk and trying to participate in that thing called the Internet that I thought was going to be such a big deal. And I knew if I didn't try this, I would regret it. And that would be inescapable." What goes unsaid is that his wife obviously decided she couldn't live with that regret either.

## EXECUTING YOUR GAME PLAN

1. Reorient your thinking when it comes to square one:

• Few people follow straight career paths anymore, and even fewer successful people do. If you have trouble believing this, start asking the people in your life you consider to be successful what route they took to get where they are. Note how many took a turn once, twice, or several times along the road.

• Remember that moving back a step or more is only advisable if it is made in service to your husband's strengths. Don't encourage him to make a change for the sake of change. Wait until you have worked out a plan together based on his strengths.

2. Help your husband identify his strengths:

• Make a list of things you think your husband does well, things he thinks he does well, and things other people in his life think he does well. Note any common items on those lists.

• Look at any long-held career dreams he may have. Even if they're not feasible, do they offer any clues as to where his strengths may lie? What about his hobbies? Are there skills he utilizes in his free time that could be applied to his work as well?

• If need be, use a strengths-testing resource like Strengthsfinder.com.

3. Help him apply his strengths:

• Discuss with your husband whether his work

utilizes his strengths. Can he approach his job in a way that allows him to apply them better? Outline ways he could begin utilizing his strengths immediately.

• If his work is truly not compatible with his strengths, weigh the risks and discuss your options. Does he need to start preparing for a new job or even a new career?

4. Practice risk management:

• If a change in direction is in order, act as his proactive partner by helping him map out the steps he needs to take and the time frame he needs to take them in. This will not only help make the process less frightening for you, it could turn a potential marriage stressor into a marriage strengthener. Your husband will feel grateful that he has a true partner he can turn to.

# 3

# Motivating Your Other Half: Turning Applause into Profit

Women are natural worriers. What stereotyping has always suggested, research has now confirmed. Not only does our brain chemistry give us a greater predilection toward worry than men, we score higher on surveys measuring the frequency of worry and are twice as likely as men to develop anxiety disorders as a result of chronic worrying.

I see this difference play out in my own marriage in a variety circumstances, but perhaps one of the starkest times is at night. It doesn't matter if the issue is some wonderful opportunity on the horizon or some looming threat, I will lie awake in bed wandering through all the possible scenarios of how the future may play out and all the obstacles that stand in the way of the outcome being a happy one. Brian, on the other hand, is usually able to set the dilemmas of the day aside and drift off to sleep immediately.

I don't think I slept more than a few hours at a time during the weeks leading up to Brian's first job in broadcasting. We had invested so much time, money, and energy getting ready to launch him into a new career. What if all that effort took us nowhere? I spent every night mentally calculating the odds he was up against: what might make station management go with another applicant, what I might have done to edit his résumé tape better, if there was anything else he could be doing to sway circumstances in his favor, and on and on and on. It was exhausting.

During this same time, Brian went on about his routine as

if it wasn't affecting him much at all. And in fact, he told me it wasn't. Yes, he was eager to land a new job, and yes, he was nervous about where we might have to move. But dwelling on it, he pointed out in a maddeningly reasonable manner, wouldn't make the phone start ringing. Better just to set it aside until a news director came calling.

But that was the difference between us—he *could* set it aside, whereas I, no matter how much I resolved to stop worrying about it, couldn't mentally let go. And the more I thought about it, the bleaker my perspective became. Within days I had worked myself into a depressed certainty that all our plans were little more than childish pipe dreams. What was worse, my constant checking and rechecking *(Are you sure you made a follow-up call to see if they received the tape? Do you think it's going to hurt you that you didn't get any severe-weather experience during your internship?)* started making Brian irritable and insecure as well. And, of course, it was all wasted energy. Within a few weeks a job offer came that turned out to be close to home and much better than we had expected.

What I went through during those bedtime sifting sessions isn't unusual for our sex. Studies have found that more than half of women are prone to what psychologists call "morbid meditation," analyzing situations to death until we are left in an extremely anxious and pessimistic state. And it is part of the reason women suffer from insomnia and depression in far greater numbers than men.

But beyond the toll this kind of worrying takes on women emotionally, it also makes us less likely to be effective motivators to our husbands. The female tendency to overanalyze, psychologist Susan Nolen-Hoeksema explains, "pollutes your thinking with negativity to the point where you are defeated before you begin." It leaves you "immobilized and demoralized."

As you might imagine, it is very difficult for a defeated, immobilized, and demoralized person to motivate someone else to strive for his best. So when we do attempt to motivate, it is often through a fearful, negative lens. What does fearful, negative motivating look like? To be blunt, it looks like nagging.

When I started asking women around me whether they encourage their husbands to fulfill their potential, almost all answered, Yes, they do. But further questioning about what exactly they say to their men returned responses along the lines of "Well, I always tell him that if he doesn't start demanding higher-profile projects he's going to keep getting passed over for promotion," or, "I told him he should've started his own business like his college friend did." Regretting opportunities lost and imagining possible threats to our futures, we employ tactics that we think of as "reminding" and "warning" but that men invariably take as nagging.

I believe the primary reason that men get so infuriated by what they call nagging is that they correctly perceive the emotional state it stems from. Nagging usually flows from a fearful suspicion that your husband isn't going to live up to the expectations you have for your life together. (At least when it's related to their careers. Nagging about hanging their pants up, taking the garbage out, and so on probably stems from a different place.)

When I'm feeling confident about our prospects, I feel almost no compulsion to remind Brian to check in with his agent or warn him how important it is he stay in shape. I do these things after dwelling on past situations that didn't go well, and negative projections of the future leave me in an anxious, critical frame of mind.

But in talking to the wives of successful men, I found that they all shared an amazing ability to let go of worry about what the outcome of their husband's ventures would be. They weren't afraid to give their men a good verbal kick in the pants when they felt it was in order, but a certain fearlessness characterized their words and actions. And their willingness to put their money where their mouths were, so to speak, inspired their husbands to conquer ever-greater challenges.

Before winning an Emmy and a Golden Globe in 2003 for his performance on the hit cable show *The Shield,* Michael Chiklis was nearing forty and being typecast in one-note chubby-guy roles. He wanted to be a leading man and knew he had the acting abilities to play such characters, but he couldn't get casting directors to consider him for those parts. "I was sort of upset about the perception in town that I was this lightweight, family-fare kind of a guy, when I knew what I was capable of doing," he recalls. After he vented to his wife Michelle about the situation one day, she was honest about what she thought was holding him back. She told Chiklis, "Look, Michael, it is not incumbent upon the studio or the networks to reinvent you. It is incumbent upon you to reinvent yourself.... You have to stop taking those roles—Mr. Roly Poly Affable Guy. You need to get in the gym. You need to change the look.... You know that you can do it. And I know that you can do it."

Had Michelle left it at that, her approach may or may not have proved effective. But she didn't. She went on to remind Chiklis what these changes could mean to his career and assured him that he was only a few adjustments away from the roles he wanted. Then, after he pointed out that taking time out to reinvent himself also meant taking time out from getting paid, she remained adamant. Says Chiklis, "My wife, God bless my Michelle, she said, 'Well, I'll sell the house. I don't care. We'll live in a little apartment. We'll do whatever we need to do.' "

While his wife was fairly blunt in her assessment of Chiklis's problem, her expression of faith in him and her willingness to back that faith up with action energized him rather than upset him. Making a commitment of that magnitude couldn't have been easy for her. Chiklis was still making a good living, even if it wasn't with the kind of jobs he wanted, and the couple had two children at home to care for. So while he may not have been thrilled to find out that his wife felt his weight and indiscriminate willingness to accept one-dimensional "nice-guy" roles were to blame for the stall in his career, he was motivated by the confidence and courage with which she was ready to help him overcome his obstacles. Once Chiklis made the changes his wife suggested, he quickly experienced a breakthrough. He was offered the gritty cop part he had always wanted, along with starring roles in big-screen summer blockbusters like *Fantastic Four*.

If you talk to most husbands, it's not their wives' genuine desire to see them do well that they resent, it is when her questioning and criticizing imply that he isn't up to the challenge. After surveying hundreds of nationally representative men, Shaunti Feldhahn discovered that the common ways a woman will try to motivate her husband actually feel like expressions of doubt to him. He then reads that doubt, however irrationally, as a sign of disrespect. "I think most women do respect in general the man that they're with; they just don't realize that throughout the day they're sending these signals that they don't," she contends. But "questioning his decisions, especially in public, makes almost any man feel like 'she doesn't respect me.' And that is his worst fear, it triggers all the insecurity that he has down deep in his heart and that sense that 'I don't know whether I can do it—I secretly doubt that I know what I'm doing—I mean if the person who knows me better than anybody else in the world doesn't believe that I can do it, then I probably can't.'" This was as true for the highly successful men in her study (those in the top income bracket with a lot of job responsibility) as it was for those who were floundering professionally. No matter how outwardly confident and self-sufficient they seemed, most of the men expressed some level of secret fear that they didn't have what it took to get all they wanted out of their careers.

When I spoke with Feldhahn about her findings, she was emphatic that, for a husband, the respect he desires from his wife in many ways relates to her demonstrations of belief in his abilities. While that may not sound crucial to a woman, Feldhahn's results showed there is nothing—not even love—that a man wants more from his wife. Out of the men she polled, 74 percent said they would rather be unloved than thought inadequate. Not too surprisingly, when women were asked the same question, they overwhelmingly chose the other option. Given that it's hard for most women to comprehend the kind of mind that would rather someone think they're good at things than love them, is it any wonder that we sometimes have trouble giving men the kind of motivation they need? So how *do* you help your husband stoke the internal fire he will need to climb his personal Everests? The answer lies in approaching the situation more as a cheerleader and less like a nag.

There's a fine line between the cheerleader and the nag. Ostensibly, they both want the same thing—the man on the field to play his best. But while a man may do what the nag wants, for the cheerleader he gives it his all and does it with a smile. The difference comes down to approach. Where the nag speaks from a place of fear (if you don't succeed, I will have to work more) or resentment (if you hadn't blown so many opportunities, we'd be in a much better situation), the cheerleader speaks from a place of unbreakable faith. Think about it. Men probably wouldn't get as pumped up watching women in short skirts lead rallies with cries of "Hey, Defense, don't blow it!" or "How come we never score?" as they do with "Go! Fight! Win!"

## The Merchants of Motivation

If you ever question whether people really need external sources of motivation to get them moving, you need only look at the publishing industry. Every other year a new motivational expert hits the scene, purporting to revolutionize the way Americans think about achievement. From Napoleon Hill's thinking and growing rich to Rhonda Byrne's secret, motivation manuals continue to do massive business. Yet if we look more closely at the titles that have graced the bestseller lists through the decades, we discover that motivating the public isn't just a big business, it is also essentially an unchanging one.

So why, then, do achievement experts continue writing, confident there will be readers enough willing to purchase yet another "conceive it, believe it, achieve it" book? Why do the bookshelves of nearly every businessperson contain a few (and frequently more) titles in the motivational genre? Simple: because human nature dictates that we will never stop looking to improve our lives. And with the exception of those rare icons of achievement who appear to be driven by some force of inner determination, most people need a little encouragement to stay on track. If they aren't getting that support from their personal relationships, then inspirational books, seminars, and CDs may be the next best option. The downside, as critics in the field of human development point out, is that while getting pep talks from a book may produce an immediate charge of ambition, it rarely translates into lasting change.

But there is another vein of motivation—one that typically goes unmined in today's overworked, overscheduled families—that *can* produce the kind of long-term drive necessary for success. As the marriage premium and Michelangelo Phenomenon demonstrate, the person most likely to inspire a man to become his best professional self isn't a life coach or even a mentor, it's his spouse. Her influence can enhance a man's self-image and help focus his abilities. Granted, that lays a lot of responsibility at a wife's feet, but it lays a lot of possibility at her feet as well. If reading the words of some distant motivational speaker is enough to spark a fresh outlook and renewed determination in a man, what might he accomplish if he had one living with him?

In 1947, during his struggle to become the first black athlete to play professional baseball, legend Jackie Robinson said of his wife, "When they try to destroy me, it's Rachel who keeps me sane." Known for his hot temper and unwillingness to mince words, it surprised a lot of people how long Robinson was able to hold his tongue while both baseball fans and players heaped abuse on him. His teammates circulated a petition to get him barred from the team; on the road he was required to board in separate, substandard accommodations; bigots mailed death threats to his home; and hostile opponents hurled racial epithets and baseballs at him.

Through it all, Jackie maintained his composure, lest an outburst ruin the chances of future black ballplayers. He later said that he would have quit during that first season were it not for his wife, who was "the one person who really kept me from throwing up my hands in despair." Wrote Robinson in his autobiography, "She felt bad because she knew I felt helpless. She hoped I realized that she knew how much strength it took to take these injustices and not fight back."

Obviously, Rachel Robinson didn't make her husband a great athlete, nor was she responsible for his innate talent. But by Jackie's own recollection, her emotional support was a crucial element in helping him desegregate the game. "We had agreed that I had no right to lose my temper and jeopardize the chances of all the blacks who would follow me if I could break down the barriers," Jackie wrote in his autobiography. His persistence paid off one spectacular day when he recalls hitting his first home run in organized baseball: "Through all the cheering, my thoughts went to Rachel, and I knew she shared my joy." Jackie's use of "we" in explaining his career reveals how deeply he recognized that breaching the color line of the major leagues was a milestone they achieved together. Jackie may have been the one on the field, but Rachel was the one giving him the strength to return to the lion's den week after week. Former American League MVP Mo Vaughn told the *Boston Globe* of his hero, "Jackie Robinson couldn't have been Jackie Robinson if it wasn't for Rachel Robinson. . . . He wanted to quit. She wouldn't let him."

While helping her husband integrate America's favorite pastime, win rookie of the year, and eventually go on to Baseball's Hall of Fame are impressive accomplishments enough, Rachel's support of Jackie had even further-reaching impact.

Years after her husband's barrier-breaking season, Martin Luther King Jr. told an aide, "Jackie Robinson made it possible for me in the first place. Without him, I would never have been able to do what I did." Looked at from that perspective, Rachel Robinson's determination to help her husband persist in the face of adversity did more than change her family's prospects, it changed the world.

What Rachel Robinson did for her man—motivating him to continue to face the ugly racism in his field and rise to the top in spite of it—doesn't require some secret and elusive set of wifely talents. But it does require the willingness to learn new ways to approach a pep talk and the mental discipline to use them rather than the fallback reactions that defeat both you and your husband.

## The Methods of Motivation

The foundation of nearly every motivational guru's plan begins with embracing optimistic thought patterns and limiting pessimistic ones. Tony Robbins calls it "changing limiting beliefs," Stephen Covey calls it a "paradigm shift," and Norman Vincent Peale simply calls it "positive thinking," but their meaning is the same: Believe you can accomplish what you set your mind to and you will be able to accomplish what you set your mind to. Overworked as the concept is with cheesy mantras like "If its going to be, it's up to me" and "Name it and claim it," on a superficial level, there is some truth in it.

The problem is that such slogans seem simplistic and, frankly, goofy, when placed up against some of the bigger challenges your husband is likely to face over the course of his career. That doesn't mean that employing optimistic thought patterns is ineffective; indeed, it is immensely effective. Studies routinely show that those with an optimistic outlook are more likely to set and achieve ambitious goals, are better able to identify and confront problems, and are more successful at finding workable solutions to those problems than people with pessimistic tendencies. They are also more adaptive at coping with stress and better able to rebound from failures—all qualities necessary for professional success.

But in recent years social science has zeroed in on more reliable and specific strategies of practicing optimism than simply thinking generic upbeat thoughts. Of course, incorporating these strategies into your interactions with your husband requires a lot more effort than chanting "In every day in every way you're becoming a better you" at him as he leaves for work, but they are also much more likely to be worth that effort.

## EMPHASIZING HIS STRENGTHS

To boost your husband's confidence you not only have to identify his unique talents, you also have to highlight those that are necessary for success in his field. Then, as you pinpoint and show appreciation for his strengths, he will recognize and appreciate them too. Note that this is a very different concept from the "You're good enough, you're smart enough, and gosh darn it people like you" approach to building confidence. Contrary to popular belief, emphasizing all-purpose self-esteem has not shown nearly the results in helping individuals achieve more in life as emphasizing their specific strengths has (in fact, some criminology studies report that prison inmates, arguably society's least successful people, tend to think extremely well of themselves).

If you have a healthy marriage, it's a good bet that your husband already knows you think he's a decent man and a likable person. So while that may be nice for him to hear, unless it relates to his goals, saying so probably won't give him a boost at the office. What he may not know, however, is that you also consider him a gifted negotiator or that you have long admired his analytical skills. Similarly, your husband may be a persuasive debater, but if he doesn't think debating is an important talent to have in his particular field, celebrating his giftedness at it isn't going to make him feel better armed to conquer his industry. If you emphasize strengths that apply to his career objectives (and that he honestly possesses), he will not only want to develop them further, he will start seeing new ways to use them to his advantage.

By the time Brian decided to go back into broadcasting, I had spent a lot of time not flattering him but genuinely praising his gift for entertaining crowds. Whenever we went to a dinner party where he told a story that had the whole table in stitches, on the car ride home I would bring up how entertaining everyone thought he was. When my friend would then call to invite us to another event because the people we met wanted to know if the "funny couple" was coming too, I would mention the conversation to him, making sure to point out that nobody thought I was particularly hilarious before we got married. These skills weren't important to the job he was already in, but they were vital in the job he was planning to pursue, so we frequently talked about how he might apply them when got his first break. As a result, Brian was pumped, primed, and excited to do whatever was necessary to get started down a new career path that made better use of his talents. I stood back, shocked, as he accomplished more professionally in six months than I'd seen him even attempt during the first three years of our marriage.

In recent years an entirely new branch of psychology, known as "positive psychology," has begun emerging that focuses on how to enhance our emotional and mental well-being rather than focusing solely on repairing psychological damage. Part of what this growing group of psychologists has found is that building a satisfying life (and, by extension, career) requires "polishing and deploying your strengths then using them to buffer against your weaknesses." Making a concerted effort to use your strengths does more than just aid in goal achievement, it also helps combat depression and contributes to lasting happiness and a sense of meaning. In the last chapter we saw how helping your husband utilize his professional strengths makes it more likely his efforts will achieve good results. But perhaps more important, positive psychology proves that it will also give him greater mental health, the foundation for being a motivated person.

## CHAMPIONING PERSISTENCE

As important as helping your husband feel good about his abilities is helping him feel good about his efforts. Experts have found that celebrating aptitude alone can lead people to feel defeated (and consequently unmotivated) when that aptitude doesn't produce immediate results. While it is crucial to verbalize your belief in his abilities (e.g., "Honey, of all the books I've read recently, I have to say, your writing is just as good if not better"), doing so might start to lose its effect if it takes him a long time to reach a goal. By placing an equal emphasis on effort ("I'm so proud of you for finishing that chapter"), regardless of the result, you help your husband celebrate the value of the attempt. This is significant, because it may take many attempts before he receives encouragement from anyone but you.

When most of us think of professional basketball players we think of the star high school and college athletes who are drafted into the NBA immediately after graduation (if they can wait that long) for astronomical pay packages. But while that is the easiest and best-known route, it's not the only way to achieve basketball stardom, as Phoenix Suns starting guard, Raja Bell, and his wife, Cindy, well know.

Though Bell harbored hoop dreams at a young age, his aspirations ran into their first roadblock after high school. None of the big schools he was interested in offered him a scholarship, so he decided to follow his father's footsteps to the University of Miami, where the coach assured him he would never play. He finally did, but only after transferring to a much smaller school. Though he did well at Florida International University, after graduation no NBA teams came calling, and Bell went undrafted. "I didn't get one invite to work out for an NBA team," he recalls. "I was a hometown kid, and not even the Heat wanted to see what I had. That was a little bit of a slap in the face."

He then signed as a free agent with the San Antonio Spurs but was dropped within months without ever playing a game. His next step was the minor leagues, playing for the Continental Basketball Association (CBA) and United States Basketball League (USBL). It was hardly a glamorous career move, as standard salaries in those leagues at the time were a mere $15,000 and $20,000 a year respectively and his first game-day duty was to wash the team's laundry. ("You want to know how to become determined?" jokes Bell. "Dirty jock-straps.") Moving to the Euroleague bumped his pay grade a bit, but it was still a long way from the life he'd dreamed of.

Throughout it all his college sweetheart Cindy was beside him in spirit if not in body, assuring him that he was making progress and would eventually reach his goal if he stayed focused on improving his game. "I could see that he was getting better all the time, and I told him the important thing was that, skillwise, he was definitely on an upward trek. And I told him that as long as that was the case, he should keep going, even though I knew it meant putting our future together on hold. It definitely took patience." She laughs, adding, "I don't know what would have happened if I had started pressuring him to forget the NBA, because Raja's a very determined person anyway. But I really believed, and told him I believed, that if he kept expanding his skills, making himself a player who could contribute on several fronts, he'd get there."

Bell's break finally came in 2001, when an injury right before the playoffs on the Philadelphia 76ers opened the door to a ten-day contract and a chance to show his hard-won proficiency on the court. Though his rise since then hasn't been meteoric, he has improved with each step, making his mark on the Dallas Mavericks, the Utah Jazz, and now the Phoenix Suns, where his aggressive guarding and clutch shooting have made him a household name among basketball fans and a lucrative endorsement figure for companies like Taco Bell.

In 2006, after an aggressive play against Kobe Bryant caught the attention of the nation, ESPN wrote of Bell, "A year ago, he was the fifth-leading scorer on a Utah Jazz team that won just 26 games. Now he's the guy responsible for The Shot [and] The Clothesline . . . that continue to shape the most exciting NBA playoffs in memory." Of her husband's sudden increase in profile, Cindy says it's no surprise. "I always felt that if Raja could maintain his determination, if he could hang in there, eventually the world would see what I've always seen."

The second key to encouraging your husband to be persistent is to respond positively when things aren't going well. The biggest difference between a nagging wife and a cheerleading motivator is probably that the nag uses guilt to keep him from letting her down in the future. She begins by reminding her spouse of what he hasn't accomplished in the past, resulting in her current disappointment. The nag believes a man is capable (she must, otherwise she wouldn't keep prodding), but her entire approach suggests that, capable or not, her husband is likely to fail her again if she doesn't maintain a constant and very vocal vigilance over his performance. The cheerleader, on the other hand, offers a clean slate by insisting that previous failures are irrelevant as anything except learning opportunities. That doesn't mean that your spouse should never consider the impact of his previous failures, but it is your job as motivator to help him dissociate them from blanket negative feelings about himself so that they don't immobilize him.

A good way to accomplish this is to help your husband employ an optimistic "explanatory style" when he experiences setbacks. One of the biggest differences psychologists have found between optimists and pessimists is that an optimist will usually explain a defeat in ways that are temporary, isolated, and impersonal. A pessimist, on the other hand, will blame setbacks on reasons that are permanent, pervasive, and personal—what former American Psychological Association president Martin Seligman calls the three "Ps": "An optimistic explanatory style stops helplessness, whereas a pessimistic explanatory style spreads helplessness. Your way of explaining events to yourself determines how helpless you can become, or how energized, when you encounter the everyday setbacks as well as momentous defeats." For example, an optimist might say that he lost a big account because his approach was too innovative for that client. This explanation is temporary (after some time passes, clients will become more comfortable with cutting-edge suggestions), it is isolated (it was only one client), and it is impersonal (it was the client's lack of vision that was the problem, not the optimist's ability to come up with good ideas). Best of all, this line of thinking gives the optimist strong motivation to try again.

In the same situation the pessimist might conclude, "I'm not a very creative thinker, so the client didn't like my idea." Obviously, responding to bad news with "I'm not creative" encompasses all three of the dreaded pessimistic Ps. It is permanent because there isn't much a person can do about not being creative; it is pervasive because such a shortcoming would affect many areas of his life and work; and it is personal because it is not that the client didn't like his idea, it is that the pessimist is unable to come up with good ones. You can see what a hindrance this style of thinking would be to developing persistence. His belief that an enduring internal defect is to blame for a failure then leads the pessimist to quit. After all, if his flaw is always going to be with him, so will the obstacle keeping him from his goal. If your husband tends toward a pessimistic explanatory style, it is vital that you help him change his negative thought patterns to find positive ways to account for failures.

It may seem counterproductive, but therapists have found that one of the best ways to begin getting their patients to see failures as opportunities for growth is to have them first identify ways in which external sources were to blame. Though at first glance it appears this would give the patients an excuse to avoid change, psychologists have found it can actually stimulate a strong desire to modify their behavior in positive ways. Explaining this seeming dichotomy, Karen Reivich of the University of Pennsylvania observes that a pessimist's tendency to explain failure with the three Ps paralyzes him from finding solutions. But by helping your husband confront setbacks by first listing causes that he was not responsible for and were beyond his control, "[he] can increase [his] ability to focus on other causes of the problem, particularly those that are more changeable." Of course I'm not suggesting that you encourage your husband to play the victim, but there is a big difference between his honestly taking stock of his behaviors to see what he could be doing better and futilely beating himself up.

If your husband suffers a serious professional setback, the first thing he probably needs to hear is that it is not a reflection of his abilities, that sometimes outside factors will work against him. Fortunately, psychologists have developed an easy three-step method for this they call disputing, which simply means arguing yourself (or in your case, your husband) into optimistic explanations for defeats. First, look for positive alternative explanations for the failure. Second, marshal evidence to support that alternative. And finally, analyze the implications of the argument you have made. Though this is a largely intuitive process people engage in whenever they argue, by consciously going through the disputation process step by step you will begin to understand it better and use it more easily. This will be especially necessary if you have a pessimistic explanatory style yourself.

After Brian had been in his new weathercasting career for about a year, he received a call from a station in a very large market wondering whether he'd be interested in a position on their weekday-morning show. Naturally, we jumped at the chance, threw some samples of his work on a VHS tape, and overnighted it to the news director. And then we heard... nothing. Weeks went by and Brian's follow up e-mails went unanswered. Finally, about a month later, I did a little investigating and discovered the station had simply promoted their weekend weather anchor into the weekday position and never bothered to follow up with any of the other candidates they had contacted. In this case, it wasn't at all difficult for me to point out ways in which Brian wasn't to blame for not getting the job.

Our *alternative explanation* was that the news director was planning to hire their weekend weathercaster the entire time but was asking for tapes as a backup and perhaps as a negotiating tactic. The *evidence* for this was that the news director must not have been taking the candidate search too seriously if he failed to respond back to the people whose tapes he solicited. Plus, we heard from acquaintances with more experience in the broadcasting business that while the salary the position paid seemed impressive to us, it wasn't at all competitive for that market. This led us to believe that perhaps management was indeed pressuring the in-house candidate to accept a substandard deal. The *implication* of these alternative explanations was that there were things going on behind the scenes at that station that Brian couldn't control; therefore, not getting the job didn't mean he didn't have the talent to be on air in a big market. If anything, he should feel encouraged even to have caught their eye. In the end, rather than feel down about the loss, he felt renewed energy thanks to their interest and hopeful that a better opportunity was on the horizon.

All this positive feeling made it easy for him, after a short time, to focus on a few of things he felt he could have done better. After we had groused together for several days about the jerks at the big station who couldn't even be bothered to respond to an e-mail, he mentioned that perhaps he had been too laissez-faire about picking his clips. He realized that he had let his impatience get the better of him and had rushed out a reel that didn't necessarily represent his best work. He also saw that he needed to start watching recordings of his show to look for areas of improvement if he wanted to make it into the biggest markets. Whereas my getting anxious and blaming him for a missed opportunity would have just made Brian defensive and angry, displaying a supportive spirit gave him room to consider how he might not miss another one in the future. Once your husband sees that you would rather be his commiserator than his accuser, he is far more likely to ponder how he might learn from a disappointing experience.

And if you need more reason to adopt an optimistic explanatory style, consider this: Over the years it has also proven to contribute to higher earnings. In the 1980s a University of Kentucky researcher decided to test the power of the positive explanatory style on first-year law students. She gave them a series of hypothetical scenarios and asked them to describe what they thought brought the events about. She then ranked each student's responses on a 5-point optimism scale—5 meaning that they almost always explained events to themselves following the optimistic pattern and 1 meaning they almost never did. Ten years later she tracked down the salaries for each of her subjects and found that for every extra point they received on the 5-point optimism scale, they brought home an additional $33,000 of annual income.

While most women will have little problem applying other motivational strategies, maintaining an attitude of optimism in the face of setbacks or stagnation can sometimes seem impossible. It's a lot easier to stay positive when your personal well-being and livelihood aren't riding on the achievements of your motivatee. But unless your husband is a very fortunate man who achieves all his goals easily, you will probably have periods of doubt when you wonder whether your efforts are being wasted.

The way to shore up your own attitude of persistence is to remember that while you may not feel it at the moment, there are masses of incontrovertible evidence that your assistance is having an effect. Then review the rewards of ongoing optimism while using the techniques above to combat your pessimistic thought patterns. Remind yourself that however permanent they may seem at the moment, most difficulties won't last forever, especially if you are employing tactics proven to be effective at eliminating them.

## Visualizing for Success

Worriers tend to magnify problems and spend an irrational amount of their energy imagining the worst that can happen. Conversely, experts recommend envisioning and expecting the best. They do so not because they believe there's some magical secret whereby meditating on the image of checks in the mail will actually cause checks to start arriving, but because, if approached correctly, positive visualization can actually galvanize people to achieve more in all areas of their lives. The problem is, the kind of positive visualization endorsed by most self-help personalities isn't the kind experts say is valuable.

There are two types of visualization techniques—outcomebased visualization and process-based visualization. If your spouse is practicing outcome-based visualizing, he is imagining that he has already attained whatever picture of success he has for himself. This is frequently the technique advocated at motivational seminars where the speaker might ask your husband to picture himself as the CEO of a Fortune 500 company, making millions of dollars, owning multiple houses, and sailing his own yacht. Not too surprisingly, these exercises are popular among readers and audiences because they're fun and they make them feel good. What they don't do, according to real research as opposed to exciting personal anecdotes, is get people any closer to achieving their goals.

In contrast, process-based visualization, which has shown outstanding results in helping people perform well professionally, is more like a mental dress rehearsal. Rather than imagining that he is an important CEO, your husband would picture himself successfully clearing the hurdles he must pass to get there, like taking on extra responsibilities to become a leader in the department he's in now or shining during corporate presentations. This exercise fulfills two major purposes: it provides the brain an opportunity to formulate plans and it walks people through the emotions they are likely to confront while executing those plans. For example, rather than focusing on how great it would be for your husband to earn a huge sales bonus, help him envision himself easily making the sales to qualify for that bonus. Once he has imagined completing each task successfully, research shows, he is far more likely to do so in real life.

Few people realize the American dream to the extent that Frank and Gloria Morgan have. Though when they started out in marriage Frank was a construction worker with a high school diploma, he was able to retire before the age of fifty, pay off his $2 million home in Phoenix, and purchase a lavishly decorated five-bedroom "cabin" in Flagstaff, Arizona, and a seaside house in Newport Beach. Their success has even had a generational impact, allowing them to employ all their children and provide them with comfortable lifestyles as well. But for the Morgans, that dream started with devastation.

In 1990 thirty-four-year-old Frank was diagnosed with stomach cancer. The doctors were not optimistic and immediately recommended he proceed with surgery and aggressive chemotherapy. In the end the medical treatments saved his life, but they also brought the Morgans further problems. Because the owner of the business he worked for had a coronary-artery bypass the same year, the company's health insurer was threatening to drop it as a client. Gloria remembers the awful result: "Something with the insurance company was that they had to insure the entire group. And the laws have changed a lot since then. But essentially, his boss told him the insurance company was saying that their policy would no longer cover both of them. He said that to maintain company coverage, someone had to go, and it was either Frank or him. So now Frank was very sick and out of a job. We were terrified."

With Gloria having always been a stay-at-home mom and Frank now seriously ill and out of work, the couple started looking for a way out of their predicament. For Gloria's part that meant going to work for the first time in her married life. Frank's solution was a bit more daunting: "I took a job as a flight attendant so we could get medical benefits," explains

Gloria, "and as sick as he was, Frank had never been one not to work, so he decided to start his own plastering company, because he didn't believe that anyone was going to hire him in his condition. We took everything we had in savings and my parents loaned us $30,000. That got us going."

To help her husband make progress during the darkest time of his life, Gloria not only pitched in physically, doing the young company's accounts and researching sales possibilities, she also helped reorient her husband's focus. "To try to take in everything we were dealing with all at once would have been too overwhelming," says Gloria. "Instead what I would do was sort of make a list of long-term goals—one-year plans, five-year plans, ten-year plans—I'm a big proponent of those. And I would say, 'Okay, after we complete this many jobs, we'll be able to pay off the medical bills, and won't it feel so wonderful not to have that hanging over our head.' Then once we'd met that goal, I'd go, 'You know, Frank, you're so good at talking to those [residential] builders, because you've worked for them and know what their concerns are; if you land two of their contracts, we could afford a cabin in Flagstaff,' which he'd always wanted."

Eventually, Gloria says, her tactic of encouraging her husband to picture the results of specific, incremental achievements helped keep his mind focused on the future he wanted rather than mired down in the problems they were dealing with in the present. "I guess it was just my way of trying to put a positive spin on the challenges we were facing," she says.

In one of the many studies that prove process visualization increases the likelihood of good results, three groups of college students were provided different instructions on how to mentally prepare for a test. The first group was told to picture themselves going through all the necessary steps of test preparation, from reviewing lecture notes to memorizing important facts, in as vivid detail as they could muster. They weren't told to carry out those steps in reality (though they weren't told not to either), they were only instructed to imagine doing them. The second group was told to meditate on the image of themselves getting a good grade on the test—how they would feel, what it would mean for their grade-point average, and so on. And the third group, the control group, was told only to record their behavior before the exam.

The group that mentally simulated test preparation tended to carry out the activities they had pictured themselves doing and, as a result, did very well on the exam. They also reported feeling less anxiety and increased confidence in their ability to pass. The group that only pictured themselves receiving an A didn't do as well, and in fact did worse than the students who were given no visualization instructions at all, indicating that outcome-based visualization may even be detrimental if practiced alone.

*The Handbook of Emotions,* a popular text in graduate and undergraduate psychology courses across the country, declares that "process simulations prepare individuals both emotionally and cognitively for the steps they must take to achieve a goal. And this preparation effectively facilitates goal attainment." Obviously, the process approach to visualization takes more work than the old "imagine winning the lottery" way, but things that produce results usually do. This doesn't mean you and your husband can't enjoy fantasizing about living in a mansion on the French Riviera. Just know that doing so probably isn't going to get you any closer to it.

Across the psychological spectrum, studies have consistently found that the human brain—of both men and women—tends to prioritize negative information and inflate fears. Therefore, when you encourage your husband to imagine himself succeeding at each step that takes him to a future in which his fondest dreams are realized, you are not painting a pie-eyed, overly optimistic portrait, you are adjusting for humanity's pessimistic leanings to paint a more realistic one.

Acting as a motivator to your husband is perhaps the simplest lesson to apprehend and the most difficult to execute. There are no checkoff lists when it comes to being your man's cheerleader and no point at which you can set aside the task as "done." Instead, it requires a daily commitment to remain positive in the face of setbacks and a willingness see the best in your man so he can see the best in himself.

One of the main reasons devotees are drawn to a motivational speaker is that he combats the "I can't" in their minds. People wouldn't get so excited over hearing someone tell them their goals were achievable if they firmly believed it already. And if you are the one convincing your husband he can realize his ambitions, he'll be all the more confident, because the woman who loves him and knows him better than anyone else believes it too.

## EXECUTING YOUR GAME PLAN

1. The first step to motivating your husband is motivating yourself. If fear and negative thought patterns are driving your interactions with him, modify your own thinking with motivational tools first.

2. In your praise and pep talks, emphasize his specific strengths as well as those that are important to his work, rather than using generic feel-good-speak.

3. Encourage him to have a positive explanatory style by helping him see how his successes are due to his efforts and talent and when his setbacks are due to outside factors beyond his control.

4. To help him avoid discouragement and burnout, celebrate his attempts as well as his victories.

5. Practice together process-based visualization rather than outcome-based visualization. Spend more time picturing him doing well at the steps it takes achieve success than on the trappings success will bring.

# Your Secret Superpower

## | Help Only You Can Offer |

Want to know whom successful men turn to first for advice on tough business decisions? Corporate consultants with advanced degrees? Former professors or other mentors? Fellow board members? Nope. They talk to their wives.

In a 2004 poll the international consultancy group Chiumento discovered that two-thirds of chief executives, managing directors, and other business leaders say that when they're facing a tough challenge at work the first person they look to for advice is their spouse. According to Bob Arnold, director of strategy at Chiumento, business leaders seek input from their wives on all sorts of work issues, including matters of top importance, like strategy, finances, and personnel. "There must be some very heavyweight conversations taking place across dinner tables," Arnold concluded after reviewing the results.

When U.S.-based Accountemps, the world's largest temporary staffing service for accounting professionals, undertook a similar study, they too found a strong preference for a wife's input. Their results weren't quite as tilted as Chiumento's, but when they asked 150 executives from the country's 1,000 largest companies whom they count on most for professional guidance, spouses again took the top spot, with 42 percent of the vote (a number that might have been higher had all the respondents been married). The runner-up response, "Mentor," came in at a distant 28 percent.

On some level it goes without saying that spouses are going to influence each other's business decisions, yet the premium today's corporate culture places on advising can leave wives feeling as if they don't have much to offer. After all, if men now have an army of advisers at work to run their decisions past, how helpful can their wives' input be? Some women feel that unless they're at the same career level or in the same field as their husbands their opinions won't be useful. But there are good reasons beyond mere proximity for why men look to their wives when they need work advice. The first is what people want most out of an adviser.

Much more than objectivity or even experience, pollsters have found that the number-one quality professionals say they look for in an adviser is trust. They need to know that person has their best interests at heart. Actor and onetime highest-paid television personality Ray Romano has said that he listens to his wife Anna above anyone else when it comes to choosing scripts, because she "comes from a place that's not about business. It's about if it's good for me."

That "it's about if it's good for me" angle is why, no matter what kind of credentials a man's colleagues, boss, or board members may boast, his wife usually still has the edge in the advising department. All those people could be hiding an agenda that negatively impacts the worth of their counsel. A wife may have an agenda as well, but hers is probably the same as her husband's—to see him do well.

The honesty factor also plays a significant role in a wife's worth as an adviser. Men in high positions often report that the people around them either aren't willing or aren't able to tell them hard truths. Their employees don't want to risk job security by pointing out unpleasant facts or suggesting how their boss could handle an issue better. Staff members can be starstruck or intimidated and don't have the clarity to see when their leader is making a mistake. But a man's other half knows him well enough to see his blind spots and is close enough to him to be frank with him about them.

Rowan Gormley, CEO of Virgin Wines, says he especially relies on his wife, Jenny, a former systems analyst who left work to care for their three children, for this kind of honesty: "Business people have a tendency to behave like sheep. Jenny has no allegiance to the flock and so can take a more independent view. It's difficult for someone whom you are paying to tell you that you are making a mistake. Jenny sometimes tells me straight out that I am completely wrong." Of course, there's an effective way and an ineffective way (read: a way sure to inspire a shouting match) to advise a man when you think he's made a misstep. But once your husband reaches a certain level in his career, you may be one of only a few people willing to offer him the candor he needs. If you don't tell him the truth, it could be that no one will.

Both of the first two factors that make wives valuable advisers spring from the relationship between spouses. You want what's best for your husband because you love him and because what's good for him is also good for you and your family. You can be honest with him because your relationship is closer and more secure than those of the people he works with. But the feature that most makes you an ideal adviser for your husband has nothing to do with the nature of the marriage relationship. Rather it's based on a skill you would probably possess whether you were married or not. And that is what you bring to the table simply by being a woman.

## Women's Advising Intuition

Hundreds of start-up companies approach International Angel Investor Institute founder Hal Nissley for backing every year. And no wonder, considering how many of his investments have proved profitable, including companies like Oracle and computer equipment manufacturer Digital Dynamics, Inc. But while the resources Nissley can draw on in deciding whether a company is worth his time and money are vast, he says his most valuable asset in his decision-making process is his wife, Juanita: "She and I have lunch or dinner at least three or four times a month with an entrepreneur. She makes the final decision," Nissley says.

It might surprise some people in the business community to know how seriously Nissley takes his wife's judgment, especially considering that she doesn't have any executive experience herself. But he maintains that it's not his wife's business insight he's interested in—it's her insight into personalities. For Nissley, the character of a company's leadership has always been a much more reliable predictor of its potential than the information listed in its prospectus. And when it comes to reading people, he says his wife "sees things I wouldn't even think to look for. . . . She seems to have a sixth sense for when someone isn't being honest with me, or when they're holding back critical information."

This might sound a bit mystical or perhaps even superstitious, but while the faith Hal Nissley has put in his wife's judgment stems from his own experience, there are universal reasons for men to seriously consider their wives' input in their business dealings. Part of what made Juanita Nissley an ideal adviser to her husband is the same thing likely to make you an ideal adviser to yours. And that is the fact that the average man is blind (or at least very nearsighted) in an area where the average woman has 20/20 vision.

Men tend to be linear, compartmentalized thinkers. They are more comfortable dealing with facts, figures, and processes than they are at dealing with personalities. Women, on the other hand, are better at handling relational issues— understanding differing sides of an argument, anticipating reactions, and deciphering motivations. This doesn't mean that some women can't be linear thinkers or that some men aren't great at reading people. It only means that because of the structure and wiring of women's brains, along with our hormonal makeup, we are, as a group, better at recognizing, predicting, and responding to emotions than men.

Only a few years ago, acknowledging these differences would have been highly controversial, if not downright politically incorrect. At that time conventional wisdom held that men and women were different because we were socialized differently—our culture treats boys and girls differently, so we exhibit one set of skills more strongly than another when we grow up. But while socialization certainly helps shape our abilities, developing research has proved that there *is* a biological difference between how each sex thinks and, consequently, what we tend to be good at.

The latest testing shows that males and females react to the world differently from the moment they are born, long before any behavioral conditioning has had time to take effect. At only one day old, male infants will look longer at a mechanical mobile suspended above them than female infants. Female infants gaze longer at a human face. One-year-old girls make much more eye contact than one-year-old boys, and girls talk earlier and have larger vocabularies during their toddler years. In fact, the evidence is so overwhelming throughout so many different branches of science that the question within the scientific community has moved from "Are there fundamental differences between the sexes?" to "What do these differences mean?"

One thing it means—at least for our purposes—is that there is a very strong likelihood that you possess abilities that could be giving your husband an edge in the workplace. If it has ever seemed to you that you know the right thing to say at the right time in an emotionally charged situation while your husband is stammering or putting his foot in his mouth, your uniquely female neural connections and brain chemistry are probably the reason.

In her groundbreaking book *The Female Brain,* neurobiologist and psychiatrist Louann Brizendine notes that among the many differences that have recently been documented between men and women's mental makeup, one of the most crucial is the fact that the female brain is far more gifted at "quickly assessing the thoughts, beliefs, and intentions of others based on the smallest hints." We pick up on everything from a change in tone to a slight shift in expression to read a person's emotional state and respond appropriately. Men, on the other hand, can have a difficult time recognizing even those emotional signals a woman would consider obvious. Brizendine says the difference between women and men in this regard is equivalent to that between an eight-lane superhighway and a small country road. And the superhighway women possess gives them "a nearly psychic capacity to read faces and tone of voice for emotions and states of mind, and the ability to defuse conflict."

I remember that in my rebellious teenage years, when I would use the occasional lie to get out of something I didn't want to do or to go somewhere I wasn't allowed, my father would almost always accept my fabrication at face value. My mother, on the other hand, would say something like "I don't know, I just feel like there's something you're not telling me." And of course there always was.

Studies show that this truth-detecting ability is not unusual among women. They often describe having "gut feelings" when something is wrong, when someone is lying, or when a friend is in trouble. Though for years it was written off as a myth, we are now beginning to understand that there are simple biological explanations for what has been called female intuition. For example, not only do our brains boast a larger communication and emotional memory center than men's, the insula—the part of our brain responsible for processing gut feelings—is bigger and more responsive as well. Estrogen also makes us more sensitive to body sensations. So when we get a funny feeling from all the emotional data we're picking up, our brains register that information immediately. Men may have a feeling that something is "off" and causing their stomach to clench or turn somersaults, but it can take them days or even weeks longer than a woman to identify the cause. In fact, some neuroscientists now believe that autism, a developmental disorder in which a person is unable to identify and respond to the emotions of others, may partly be the result of overexposure to testosterone in the womb. They believe that an autistic brain is really an extreme male brain, and indeed the disorder affects far more boys than girls.

But even setting aside the amount of subtle nonverbal communication men miss, they also don't pick up as much outright communication as we do. You know the cliché that men don't listen as well as women? Well, they don't. Or better stated, they can't, because they don't have as many aural neurons—cells designed to process sound—as we do. And when they are listening, MRI scans show that men typically engage only the left side, or the logical, linear side of their brain. Women use both the logical left and the intuitive right, so not only do we grasp more of what other people are saying, we also remember it more accurately for a longer period of time.

All of this is why even accomplished, savvy businessmen who are confident in most situations can feel flummoxed by emotion-based problems. First, they are probably having a hard time deciphering what the conflict is. And second, once they do, they may have difficulty deciding the best way to handle the situation. Because men's brains frequently don't register subtle emotional cues, they can let a problem fester, unaware of it, until it boils over. Some of the most successful men in the world have admitted that while they know exactly how to increase profitability for their company, they often have no idea what they've done to offend a colleague or how to remedy an awkward situation until they talk it over with their wives. By the same token, a man may write off comments or behavior that reveal clearly malicious intent until his wife apprises him of the threat looming on the horizon.

It is for this special ability to read people that Rowan Gormley says he asks his wife about personnel issues and to meet anyone he is considering hiring. "I might be impressed by someone because they have an MBA or because they worked at [a large, impressive company], but she doesn't consider them in those terms." Instead, he says, she comes at things from a more instinctive angle. "I wouldn't ask her if we have filed our corporation tax correctly or what we should do about our marketing strategy. But if somebody was being inappropriate or unreasonable, I would ask her, 'How would you react to this?'"

Looking back at the marriage premium, this could partly account for why men benefit from their wives professionally far more than women benefit from their husbands. Over the last thirty years, as women have entered the labor force in larger numbers, they were taught to sharpen skills that come more naturally to men, like bottom-line strategizing and aggressive negotiating. Men, on the other hand, weren't equally required to develop the emotional intelligence that comes so naturally to women. Perhaps someday they will be, but in the meantime, being his eyes in areas where he is blind can give your husband the best of both genders' strengths.

## Knowing Your Husband

It is not just your ability to read other people that can make you an effective adviser to your husband, it is also your ability to read him—something you probably do better than anyone else in his life.

One of the interesting things experts like Dr. Brizendine have noted during their years of observing interactions between men and women is that wives often know when something is troubling their husbands before they do. Brizendine describes how one of her patients, Jane, recognized that her husband wanted to make a career change even before he was consciously aware of it.

Jane began to notice that whenever her husband Evan would talk about going to the office, his tone would grow more hesitant and his jaw would tighten. When she told him that it might be time for him to start investigating other job opportunities, he insisted that he wasn't near considering any such thing. But a short time later Evan realized that he did want to take his career in another direction, he just hadn't known it yet.

A similar situation occurred to Richard Parsons when he was considering his first major career transition, going from being a corporate lawyer to taking the helm of Dime Bank:

*The guy who was running the Dime was a client of mine. He'd encouraged me to apply for the job on two previous occasions, and both times I'd said no. Then he came back a third time and I decided to talk to Laura seriously about it because sometimes you can mentally get yourself so wrapped up in these things—overwrought, so to speak— that you stop making any progress in your thinking. So I asked her, "What do you think?" And she said, "I don't know, it just seems to me that you've gotten a little stale in what you're doing. You don't seem as engaged by it. And to me it seems like you need to take on a new challenge." I asked her to explain what she meant and she said, "Well, let's be honest. Right now you're really just a high-priced baby sitter." (I was a lawyer still, but I'd stopped litigating because I was working for a lot of corporations and high-net-worth individuals.) She told me, "I don't know if this is the right challenge, but I know that you need one." Suddenly I realized, you know what? She's right. I have gotten stale. I'm not enjoying myself. So I accepted the position.*

While Parsons felt that his wife's belief in his abilities played a part in her encouraging him to take the job, he's convinced that her intimate knowledge of him and her ability to read his emotional states was the bigger factor. "Well, she probably does have more confidence in me than I do in my-self, but to tell you the truth, I don't think she was even oper-ating on that level. She just was telling me what she was reading in me, which was, 'You seem kind of bored with what you're doing now. It's lost some of its magic and charm for you and you would benefit from taking on a new challenge." Later, as he was considering yet another major career leap, Parsons once again found that Laura's ability to read not just other people but also him was a valuable component in his decision-making process.

When then–Time Warner CEO Gerald Levin first ap-proached Parsons about taking over his role, Parsons insisted that they first schedule a dinner for four—the two men and their wives. In part it was because he trusted Laura's judg-ment on other people, but it was also because he trusted her judgment on him. "Sometimes," he points out, "you want your wife to meet all the parties involved not just so she can tell you whether she thinks the other people are honest or have integrity. It can also simply be a matter of wanting her opinion on how well the other individuals' working style will fit with yours. With Levin, I knew it wouldn't work if he and I didn't work well together. And once you make a decision like that, it's like you're on a bullet train and you have to ride it until the end, so I very much needed Laura's input."

Despite their very different leadership styles, Laura deter-mined that they could work well together, and by almost any account she was right. Parsons was able to fend off the cor-porate raiders who were beginning to circle around the ailing media conglomerate and return the company to financial sta-bility. So when using your facility for analyzing your hus-band's colleagues, remember to factor in how his personality will mesh with theirs to contribute to his success.

## Knowing His Business

Now that we know why no one can be the adviser to your husband that you can, is there anything else you can do to improve your effectiveness at it? Yes. You can get to know his business. While there is a certain knack some people have for reading others and giving good advice, there is no way to get around the value of understanding what your husband does at work every day if you are to offer him sound counsel.

There is perhaps no filmmaker working today who hasn't been in some way influenced by the work of Alfred Hitchcock. His movies changed the face of the entertainment industry. But what few probably realize is how much they have also been influenced by Alma Hitchcock, who was throughout her life her husband's closest adviser. Her opinion meant more to him than anyone else's, claims the couple's daughter, and she advised him on "script material, casting, and all aspects of production." Alma's own artistic vision was so integral to Hitchcock's work, actor and film historian Charles Chaplin Jr. has asserted that "the Hitchcock touch had four hands. And two of them were Alma's."

One of the reasons Alma was able to provide such valuable counsel to her husband was that she took a vital interest in his work and understood every aspect of the filmmaking business. A particular instance Patricia Hitchcock O'Connell recalls is *The Pleasure Garden*, the first feature film that her father directed to completion. It was an important turning point in Hitchcock's career, and he knew it. If this film went well, it could mean bigger budgets on higher-profile projects. If it didn't, it could mean many more years on short films or as someone else's assistant director. Understandably nervous, he looked to his wife for advice on every detail. "After each shot he would discreetly turn to Alma and ask, 'Was that all right?' My mother was the only one ever to see that side of Daddy." After shooting, Hitchcock involved Alma in editing the final cuts. And in the end their collaboration was responsible for the official launch to Hitchcock's illustrious career, with the London *Daily Express* declaring Hitchcock "the young man with the master mind."

It's impossible to act as a strong adviser without taking an interest in your husband's industry. Alma Hitchcock had an advantage in that she came out of a filmmaking background herself. But for many wives that is not the case. Sandy Weill, billionaire investor and former CEO of Citigroup, is notorious for listening to his wife Joan's counsel about business matters above anyone else's. Her credentials that qualify her for this role? She was a kindergarten teacher and a stay-at-home mom. But her lack of formal business training never deterred her from showing intense interest in her husband's daily activities and the workings of Wall Street, where he carried them out.

When business reporters talk to people around Sandy Weill to discover the source of his success, they often voice their admiration for Joan. She has been called "the best merger he ever made," "the ultimate corporate wife," "Weill's lieutenant," and his "chief regulator." His successor as Citigroup CEO commented that "there are very few major business decisions that he doesn't ask her opinion on." And Weill himself has said, "I would have had no career without my wife. We made all the decisions together."

True to form, Joan was particularly instrumental when it came to advising her husband about people. In fact, at a pivotal business juncture, Weill called negotiations to a halt until Joan could meet and offer her opinion on the parties involved. But to ensure that her advice was as valuable to her husband as possible, Joan Weill didn't just rely on instinct, she ensured she understood as much about her husband's work as possible. It was thanks to this that during crucial power plays, she was able to offer sophisticated advice on internal corporate politics. When Weill considered giving up the CEO title of his first company to American Express for an executive position and a seat on their board, his wife warned him not to. "Shearson [the first company Weill founded] is your power base. Don't give up your anchor." When she overheard reporters at press gatherings misrepresenting Citigroup developments, she was able to quickly correct them, and warn her husband that he needed to clarify certain points publicly. In fact, Joan Weill knew so many details of her husband's business that a therapist she was seeing was able to use her confidences to commit, unbeknownst to her, insider trading.

Based on his own experience, Sandy Weill eventually came to have such high regard for spouses' insights that one of the first changes he implemented at every company he took over was inviting them to sit in on company meetings.

## Advising from Ignorance: The Smart Dummy

Sometimes, however, your *unfamiliarity* with a particular situation can also be a boon to your husband. Microsoft often tests potential new products through a system called the "smart dummy." The idea is that if you expose your decision-making process to someone who is generally intelligent though ignorant of the specifics (a smart dummy), that person will frequently ask insightful questions and bring up important points that experts overlook by virtue of being too close to the subject. Parsons says that over the years his wife has been particularly helpful to him in the "smart dummy" capacity. "She may not be as well versed in the media business or the banking business as I am," he says, "but she's smart enough that I can expose her to problems and issues and she will ask very sound baseline questions that cause me to think about it in a different light. I mean, I may have talked to four guys who are doing the same thing I'm doing and we all started at level six and moved up from there and we forgot to go back to level one and build up to level six again."

Of course, for your husband to benefit from your insights you have to know how to talk to him about his job so that he's inclined to respect your advice. If you aren't able to communicate your counsel to him in such a way that takes into consideration the way his brain works and the information processes that are particular to him as a man, you're just as likely to annoy or anger him as to help him.

## How to Speak So He Will Hear

If your marriage is anything like mine, sometimes it seems like there is no way to offer a suggestion or any meaningful help without upsetting your husband. Many arguments with Brian used to start with him saying, "It's not that I mind you making a suggestion, it's the *way* you make it," and me throwing up my hands in exasperation, yelling, "Well, apparently there is no right way to approach you about these things!" Eventually I figured out there was.

Deborah Tannen, a linguistics professor at Georgetown, has made a career out of studying the way men and women behave in conversation. What she has found is that, true to the differences in our brain makeup, women converse to build a sense of community while men speak to establish status and impart information. Not surprisingly, then, women tend to weary quickly of the information-saturated lectures men often give, while they have little tolerance for our attempts to bond through questioning and sharing personal experiences. This is because men speak in what Tannen calls "report talk" and women speak in "rapport talk." And each gender is apt to misinterpret the intentions behind the other's style.

While women in conversation prefer a circular approach to advice, like the gentle coaching of a line of questioning or introducing the subject with a personal experience, men tend to prefer straight-shot declarations, followed by supportive arguments. I tend to think of it terms of planes. Women in conversation are more like the large commercial airliners that circle around the airport before finally coming to a relatively gentle landing. Men in conversation are like fighter jets—they take off in an abrupt straight line and end in the same way. And they are much more sensitive to what they perceive as being "talked down to."

Whether because of nurture or nature, women usually don't want to be seen as overly forceful or opinionated. We want to show that we understand that this is a conversation of equals sharing ideas and experiences and that our suggestions are only that, suggestions. At the same time, however, we typically believe our suggestions to be right (otherwise we wouldn't have them in the first place). So to avoid seeming to be giving orders, we phrase them as gentle interjections, questions, and musings.

What may come as a shock to some women is that men find a comment like *"I think that's a mistake, and because of factors A, B, and C, I think it would better for you to . . ."* less bossy and authoritative than *"Well, have you considered A, B, or C factors? Don't you think it might be better if you . . . ?"* To us, this only sounds polite. To men, it sounds manipulative. Either they feel that you are trying to be deceptive about your opinion or they feel impatient and wish you would get to the point. As my husband told me, when I ask him, *"Don't you think* you *should . . . ?"* or, *"Do you think it might work better if . . . ?,"* he feels as though I am a mother trying to coach her child into having some sense. That doesn't mean you can't ask a question when it is genuine, but when it is a question designed to maneuver him toward the answer you already have, most men are on to it and resent it.

So how do you go about offering your counsel? First remember that husbands usually don't express themselves for the sake of expression nearly as much their wives do. Most times, if he brings up the subject with you, he expects you to have (and voice) an opinion. So rather than saying, "Don't you think it would be better if you put yourself in the running for the larger accounts?," you would use the direct but still respectful approach of "I think you're ready to take on bigger accounts." And then make your case: "One, you have handled several medium-size projects extremely well, and all your clients have reported being very satisfied with your work. Two, you have the most experience of the executives at your level. Your firm's probably going to be looking to promote from within soon, and it will show you have the confidence and initiative to handle those larger responsibilities." State your opinion, then outline the factors that led you to form it. And, remembering that men prefer systems and ordering to meandering conversation, lay your advice out in simple, connected steps. Because of A, B, and C, I think you should do D.

But the best way to get your husband to seriously consider your advice is to offer it a way that respects the fact that the final decision is his. If he isn't worried that you're going to be angry or offended if he ultimately decides not to take it, he's much more likely to hear you out. And if advising is a new prospect to you and your husband, it may take time for you both to get comfortable with the idea. But it is more than worthwhile to make that effort. Let your husband know why you are becoming more interested in his work and how you'd like to be of assistance to him. As long as you make it clear that your advice is just that—advice that he is ultimately free to take or leave—it is the rare man who won't appreciate the value of it.

## EXECUTING YOUR GAME PLAN

1. Recognize the unique value you hold for your husband just by being a woman. If this concept is new to you both, explain to him (in a noncondescending manner) how your brain makeup helps you to see things he often can't.

2. Trust your instincts and listen to your intuitions— if you experience strong feelings about a person or situation related to your husband's work, explore where those feelings are coming from.

3. Seek to understand his business to make your insights more valuable. But . . .

4. Don't be afraid to ask questions or offer opinions even when you aren't familiar with or don't fully understand a particular situation. Occasionally your ignorance can be an asset.

5. Share your intuitions in a direct, specific manner. Though your opinion may be primarily based on emotional data, try to frame it for your husband with concrete support.

# 5

# Using Your PR Savvy to Increase Household Cash Flow

Women in the corporate world often complain that the system still tends to reward qualities that favor men. Aggressiveness, competitiveness, issuing orders—most women report that they aren't as comfortable exhibiting these "masculine" characteristics as their male colleagues are. But there are two vital business skills that women often have an advantage in: networking and public relations.

If you haven't had much experience in the corporate world or if your professional background hasn't involved networking or relating with the public in any official capacity, your initial reaction to this chapter's title may be, "But I don't have any PR savvy! And I've never had to do any networking." Not to worry. The first thing to know is that we all network and practice public spin (or presenting the best possible image to particular people, which is all PR is at its core) in our daily lives. The second thing to know is that as a woman, you're probably naturally more adept at it than your husband.

Research shows that women have far wider social circles and more friends than men, which is no surprise considering that the distinctive way women speak to one another allows them to form connections in short spans of time. Think of the little things women say that help them bond with one another quickly—revealing difficulties and offering recommendations, for example. Can you imagine one man, after finding out that they both have toddler-age children, asking another if he and his wife are struggling with potty training too? Or even further, imagine the other one responding, "You know, we were, but then I read this wonderful book. You've got to read it! I'll get the name for you."

Language experts observe that the reason men would be unlikely to have this exchange (beyond the fact that they're rarely in charge of potty training) is that where women's conversation patterns are based on establishing intimacy, men speak to establish hierarchies—to discover where everyone is on the status scale (e.g., *"Nice to meet you, Bill. So Tom tells me you're a cardiologist."*) To admit that he is having trouble with a fatherly duty would make a man feel that he is putting himself in an inferior position. And being an enthusiastic audience to the other man's advice would suggest to the second man that his superior knowledge gives him a higher social ranking. We laugh because two women having the same conversation would never look at it this way. But after studying tapes of groups of men who have just met, specialists note that they spend a lot of time "finding out who [is] best informed about movies, books, current events, politics, and travel as a means of sizing up the competition and negotiating where they [stand] in relation to each other." Groups of newly introduced women, on the other hand, spend their time "gaining closeness through self-revelation." Or as one Fortune 500 executive put it to me, "Women are so often worried about 'what will people think of me?' Guys don't do that. They're more concerned with 'who's better than me?'"

This doesn't mean that men's conversations are rancorous or that they aren't having fun—as hard as it can be for us to understand, men often enjoy this sort of conversation-as-competition. But the male speaking style does mean that they aren't as likely to talk to each other again after that day, let alone initiate a friendship, as women are.

While examining the unique way women network, a reporter for *The Wall Street Journal* discovered that "women prefer to develop relationships in more intimate talks and then get down to business, whereas men focus on business and may never form personal bonds.... Unlike, say, a men's poker group, the game [for women] can take a back seat to the conversation. 'You talk about your thoughts and feelings and break down barriers,' says [one woman]. 'Once in a while, the game gets played.'"

It is this "nonwork" connection that can make female networking so effective. If half the networking equation is making contacts, the other half is maintaining and maximizing them. Peter Astley-Sparke, CEO of a software company that specializes in relationship-management programs, says that it has been his experience that women's predilection toward quality over quantity gives them the upper hand in forming networks:

> *It's the old preoccupation: questions from our male customers tend to center on the size of their network, those from women on techniques for deepening their relationships.*
>
> *By way of example, here's a typical support request from "Mike":*
>
> *"I've just downloaded your free trial of Cortege and was wondering how best to organize my network. I have 2,400 close contacts and about 3,200 others—what would you recommend?"*
>
> *My immediate reaction was to reply:*
>
> *"5,600 contacts is not a network, it's a mailing list...."*
>
> *Research clearly demonstrates what most women seem to know intuitively: that a large network of weak*

*links is far less valuable (in personal, career or economic
terms) than a much smaller network of strong ones.*

Not only are women better at turning contacts into
friends, they make more effort at sustaining those friendships. Women see one another more often and share more of
what is going on in their lives. Those wives who raise their
"networking consciousness" on behalf of their husbands are
likely to find that their conversations with female friends
produce an extraordinary amount of helpful information.

Remember Michael Chiklis, the Emmy–winning actor
from *The Shield* whose wife helped him by being a strong
motivator? During the time that he was struggling to change
his image in Hollywood, Michelle Chiklis struck up a friendship with a woman at her daughter's Gymboree class who
happened to be married to a screenwriter. While waiting for
their kids to wrap up their classes, they got to talking about
their husbands, and Michelle asked the woman what projects
hers was working on. The friend replied that he was writing
a pilot that centered on a courageous but deeply compro-
mised cop in L.A. It sounded exactly like the kind of show
that could take Chiklis's career in a new direction.

Michelle asked her friend if she could get her husband to
pass along the script to Chiklis. She complied. Chiklis loved it,
and after convincing the screenwriter that he could handle the
violent, complex character, the part was his. By his own admission, Michael Chiklis probably would never have been considered for the Emmy- and Golden Globe–winning role that
changed his career had it not been for his wife's connections.

The other feminine characteristic that can make networking especially productive is our disposition toward "team-
work." It may be because of biology or it may be because girls

are raised to please others whereas boys are raised to prize independence, but women as a group embrace a more collaborative approach to life. Studies show that for years our understanding of the human stress response—fight or flight—was based solely on *male* stress responses. We now know that female stress response is better characterized as "tend and befriend." In early civilizations, it was impractical for women to try to fight off male enemies with superior strength, and it was often impossible to flee from danger with young children in tow. This led women to form groups that pooled their resources to help guarantee the safety of all. When faced with challenges, women still rely on collective rather than individual efforts because our social connections have historically provided us with better protection than shows of strength or running away.

This especially reveals itself when applied to networking. Listen to how a man and woman each responded to the *Wall Street Journal*'s question on gender and networking. A female lawyer complained that the men she contacts "often dismiss, patronize, tune out or compete with her. . . . 'I don't usually have these problems when networking with other women. By and large, the women I contact are more receptive, interested, collaborative and better prepared to receive, as well as provide, information.'"

After hearing this charge, a male management consultant didn't deny it, but instead argued that men are often right to withhold assistance: "As a job-search or career-development technique, networking is about exchanging information that represents enormous clout and leverage. Those who have it can't be expected to hand it over readily." And there it is: the collaborative versus the competitive point of view in Technicolor.

In my own work I have found that the idea that women follow through where men fail to respond when a friendly request is made of them is more true than not. In fact, I ran up against this issue repeatedly while writing this book. Whenever I called on my female friends—or even friends of my female friends—to connect me with good couples to interview, almost every one of them got back to me quickly with several candidates. Since women's networks are mostly made up of other women, the contact information they provided was usually for the wife. When I contacted her, she almost always responded to me in a matter of days, even if it was only to politely decline my request.

Going through the men in my social circle was like pulling teeth. Whether it was male friends, business associates, or even male relatives, I would have to leave several messages before they got back to me. Some never did. True to form, those who did offer suggestions for interview subjects typically gave me the names of other men. Contacting these men, with referrals, produced even more dismal results. After I left numerous messages for them, only a handful ever responded. To give it a percentage, I would say I had about an 80 percent return on the women I contacted as a result of referrals from other women and only a 15 to 20 percent return on the men.

If I had to guess at the reason, it would be this: the men heard that a writer was calling to interview them for a book about how the husband-wife dynamic plays into business. It had nothing do with their specific field, and I had little to reciprocate with in the favor bank. Therefore, although few said no, few felt any internal pressure to get around to saying yes. The women, on the other hand, were helpful for the sake of being helpful. For good or for ill, this is part of the female identity, and it is part of what can make our connections so valuable.

You may be wondering how much good you can do for your husband by networking with other women. You don't want to limit your efforts to one gender, and as we'll see in a moment, reaching out to other women often breaks down obstacles conventional networking methods can't. Women have an impressive ability to make things happen for one another (not the least of which is that while a man may feel no compunction to respond to a call for help from an acquaintance, he isn't likely to ignore a request made by his wife). By drawing on the bonds of sisterhood, you may open doors for your husband that he wouldn't have known existed otherwise.

Now let's look at public relations. With an estimated 70 percent of the industry comprising females, it is one of few fields in which women are the majority. And with good reason. Just as we saw with advising, women's ability to read others' emotions quickly with little information gives us a leg up in situations that require us either to present a positive image or to engender positive feelings. We can put ourselves in another person's shoes and intuit what they will respond to better than most men.

Frank Wylie, former president of the Public Relations Society of America, credits women's superior communication skills for their dominance in PR, noting that "our society places a greater communication burden-opportunity on women, teaching them to listen and thus begin to understand communication's most basic aspects. . . . They communicate, observe, listen and write better." Pointing out that women use an average 7,000 words a day and five tones of speech, while men use only 2,000 and three tones, Scott Haltzman, psychiatric specialist in men and communication, concurs. "Men are talk-impaired, relatively speaking," he states. So if there is something positive about your husband that he needs to convey to an audience, there is a good chance that you will find a more persuasive and subtle way to say it than he will.

Darlene Schmitt estimates that after she started working with her husband Perry in his real estate business, his revenues grew by 65 percent. Though Darlene performs numerous tasks that enhance her husband's profitability, she says one of the most effective is her skill at promoting him. "Perry is incredibly knowledgeable and experienced," she says, "but he never really went out of his way to specifically let prospective clients know that. Either they picked up on it from talking with him or they didn't." That changed when his wife officially became his partner.

"One of the things I started doing to make it clear to clients how well respected [Perry] is in our industry was to let them know that other people in our business come to him when they're looking to sell their house or buy investment properties. We have a client whose own daughter is a real estate agent and he still uses Perry. The mortgage lender in our office and all the people in the title company know countless Realtors, but they still come to Perry. He doesn't feel comfortable bringing this up with new clients. But I do, and I can definitely say it's made a difference to our bottom line."

The problem when it comes to both networking and PR is that few wives recognize how valuable their abilities are in these areas and how to channel them to benefit their men. I have a friend who, though she would never describe herself with these business terms, is the ultimate networking and public relations specialist. She is bubbly and effusive, and always seems to have some event or another to attend. She is more than an extrovert—she is a charming, warm extrovert. She is also a consummate connector. People who are close to her typically end up being good friends with one another as well. And she champions her friends' talents so that more than a few them have made profitable business alliances thanks to her introductions.

Yet she rarely uses this amazing magnetism on behalf of her husband. A high-level executive at a publicly traded company, he tends to be more quiet and reserved. Perhaps because of his intimidating background and the magnitude of his work responsibilities, he doesn't have anywhere near the social circle his wife does. But because she doesn't consider herself a businessperson, she underestimates how valuable her contribution might be. And it's not because her husband doesn't value her gifts. When I mentioned the topic of my book to him, without any solicitation he revealed that he wished his wife were more willing to accompany him on business trips and attend functions where her innate lovability might work in his favor.

I don't think it's because she doesn't care about her husband's work needs or isn't willing to help that she doesn't comply. I think it's because she truly does not believe that she could make much of a difference. She is wrong.

## Building a Network

### LIKE CHARITY, NETWORKING BEGINS AT HOME

It has been estimated that only 30 percent of job openings are posted in professional journals or on job sites like Monster.com and that 90 percent of all executives landed their jobs through networking. Most people, with a reasonable amount of diligence and responsibility, can rise to mid-level positions. But to move higher, it clearly helps to know people.

The good news is that you probably know more people than you think.

Part of the reason that the idea of networking sounds so awful to many wives, particularly those who have never been in the business world or have been a long time away from it, is that they fear networking will interfere with their schedules and that it will feel artificial and self-serving. They picture themselves running around trying to meet important people of whom they can ask favors. Understandably their reaction is that this would be too uncomfortable and time-consuming a prospect, no matter how many doors it might open.

There's a place for chatting up important figures in your husband's field, but those occasions probably won't come up too often. And because your most productive networking will usually spring from people you already know, that's all the more reason to get your feet wet in familiar waters.

A couple months before my husband Brian's first broadcasting contract was up, we started preparing to make his next move. By this time he had an agent to locate job openings, send tapes, and make follow-up calls to news directors. But even with an agent, there's no guarantee that a news director will actually look at your tape. In competitive markets, a station will receive hundreds of tapes per opening, and many go unwatched. So when a position opened up in our hometown, I wanted to make sure Brian was given serious consideration. I worked down my female networking chain, first calling my sister-in-law. "Do you have any connections to anyone at that station?" I asked.

"Well, I don't," she admitted, "but my friend Jill knows a part-time producer there. She cut back to a couple days a week last year after she had a baby. But I think Jill said she's still pretty influential around their newsroom."

I asked my sister-in-law whether, despite the fact that I didn't know Jill outside of a couple of introductions, she wouldn't mind calling her friend to see if she could help us. True to what I'd noted about female responsiveness, Jill immediately let us know that she'd put a call in to her friend. Within two days, the friend contacted me to let me know she'd be happy to help and that we should send Brian's tape directly to her. She then sent follow-up e-mails to tell me that she'd played the tape for management during their weekly meeting and that they thought Brian was terrific. It didn't end up being the right job for us, but because of my networking we knew that he was seen and consequently liked—something even his agent couldn't ensure.

To make the most of your personal relationships in a business sense, you have to be in tune enough with your husband's career goals to know when a friend might be able to offer an opportunity. And you have to be willing to ask her for help.

At the beginning of his career as a stockbroker, Sandy Weill was so shy he couldn't land any clients. His wife Joan gave him a jump start by calling on friends, neighborhood acquaintances, and even old boyfriends to invest with her husband. Once Weill gave them a good return on their money, the word got out about what a savvy investor he was. But that couldn't have happened if his wife hadn't done a little networking magic to start with.

If you're concerned that it's going to feel awkward or false to start using your contacts to help your husband professionally, consider being upfront with your friends from the outset. There is no reason not to discuss what you're trying to achieve through networking. Tell them what you've read about how wives can have a significant impact on their husbands' careers through networking and that you're giving it a try. You might be surprised to find how many other wives in your circle want in on the idea.

Men have long had formalized social groups whose secondary purpose was to advance one another's careers. If groups of women, who already have strong relationships, endeavor to do the same on behalf of their spouses, they are likely to find that their girlfriends are at least as open and enthusiastic to the idea of giving one another's husband's a hand as the old boys' club once was and often still is. Wives and mothers have a long history of pooling their resources to help one another out with child care, education issues, and charitable efforts. Networking for their husbands' sake essentially takes the same skills and broadens them into a new area. And because status is less of a concern for women, we don't see ourselves as losing face by asking for help or a favor when a friend is a in a position to give it. As a result, women are both more likely to ask for help and more likely to give it—the complete circle of networking.

## Networking and PR by Default

Sometimes wives practice strong networking and PR skills on their husband's behalf just by showing up. One of the benefits of marriage is that at social functions you always have a partner to play off who can add a new dimension to your personality that your colleagues aren't familiar with. Have you ever met a gruff, seemingly imposing man, then met his gracious, amiable wife? Your entire opinion of him changes.

Kathleen Matthews laughs about how often people comment on her ability to transform their view of her famously cantankerous husband from growling grizzly to teddy bear.

Though Chris Matthews's influence as moderator of MSNBC's *Hardball* is responsible for many of the invitations they get to important political events, she concedes that once they arrive, "[people] like him a lot more because of me. . . . I think they would say that I round out a lot of his hard edges." She says that while people "always get the authentic Chris," her presence can serve to soften him.

I have had wives tell me that their husband doesn't really need them at certain work-related functions and he doesn't mind going alone. That may be, but what he minds and what serves to raise his profile in his profession are two different things. In that same vein I've had stay-at-home moms tell me they don't go to their husband's functions because they don't enjoy mixing with corporate moms who only talk about work and act superior to them. And I've heard working moms say they don't like chatting with full-time mothers who only talk about their kids and act superior to them (it should go without saying that if people come away from a conversation with you feeling like you think you're superior, you're not networking or relating to them very well). These defensive feelings that are so often manufactured by our media can be difficult to navigate, but remember what your purpose is— not to defend your life choices but to further your husband's business opportunities.

Many successful men become so because they have a presence in their field. Part of this stems from having a strong track record, but even with a strong record it's easy to fly under the radar these days. In almost any business those who do well have names and faces that are familiar to large numbers of their peers. This is made all the more likely if you are out meeting, greeting, and creating a positive impression alongside him.

As a stay-at-home mother of three, attending conventions, work dinners, and other events didn't come naturally to Dawn Campbell, whose husband is COO at a commercial construction company. But by doing it, she says, she learned its value. "I was a second-grade teacher before I left work, so the idea of the corporate world was intimidating to me. I felt like, what was I going to do, talk *Good Night Moon* with real estate attorneys? But what [my husband] Jimmy did, and I'm not sure many husbands do this, was make it clear that he wanted me to go to these things not to discuss work, but so people could get to know him better. You feel more comfortable with people, and I think you want to give them your business more, when you feel like you know them. . . . And my husband doesn't really have that outgoing a personality. He says that it's easier for him to make social contacts if I'm with him." She adds that wives who aren't experienced at accompanying their husbands to business functions will probably be surprised to find out how little people actually want to talk business. "People usually prefer to talk about their kids, their hobbies, and stuff like that. I think that's another reason why people like having their spouses there—it gives them space to talk about something other than work."

As an addendum to those thoughts, though, to continue being a social asset to your husband, it's crucial that you not fall into a networking rut. The easiest thing to do at the company picnic or Christmas party is to stick with the people you already know. As the wife, you don't have many networking opportunities within his business, so you need to make the most of them as they come up. Make it a point to introduce yourself and converse with as many people as you politely can rather than staying seated at a table with a familiar crowd. If your husband is an employee, don't shy away from saying hello to his boss. If he's the boss, take a few minutes to get to know his employees.

Most important, remember that however lighthearted the function, if it involves your husband's work, you are there as a sort of ambassador, and part of public relations is representing him well.

Overstock.com CEO Patrick Byrne says he uses company gatherings as an opportunity to learn more about his employees from their spouses. And what he learns isn't always flattering. On one occasion he discovered that his hunch that one of his executives was undermining the others was correct by chatting with the man's wife. She spent the entire conversation running her husband's colleagues down. "I can generally tell what a guy is saying at home from what his spouse says after a glass of wine or three," Byrne noted wryly.

Home is probably where your husband vents about his job and the frustrations he may have with it. Given how embarrassingly many spouses behave at functions, you have a leg up just by remaining friendly and casual. When you attend events as a couple, you increase the chances that you will create positive impressions and form mutually beneficial relationships.

## Big-Fish Networking

This may never happen to you, but lightning does occasionally strike, and if it does you don't want to fail to catch it. If your husband's in the market for a new job or looking to land a large client and an opportunity presents itself, it's worth taking a shot.

In 1985 country star Alan Jackson was still living in New-
nan, Georgia, the small town where he'd been born and married his high school sweetheart Denise. While he held a variety
of jobs like car sales and construction during the day and
played at local bars with his band, Dixie Steel, at night, his wife
Denise worked as a flight attendant for Piedmont Airlines.
While on the job in Atlanta one evening, Denise spotted Glen
Campbell waiting for a flight. Rather than let a golden opportunity go by, she screwed up her courage and walked over to
him, told him what a huge fan she was, and asked if he had any
advice on the first steps a person should take to break into the
music business.

During the ensuing conversation she told Campbell what
an incredible talent her husband was and offered him a
demo tape. In return Campbell gave her his business card,
and said that if he liked what he heard, he might be able to
hire Jackson as a songwriter for his music publishing company. Though it took another year of polishing his songwriting skills before Campbell officially hired him, once on staff
Jackson excelled in the role and over the next three years
penned several hit songs for better-known country stars before getting a chance to record his own album in 1989. Since
that first record, Jackson has gone on to sell 40 million al-
bums and score more than thirty number-one singles on the
Billboard country charts.

Denise Jackson used a time-honored networking tactic in
her approach to Campbell. She didn't rush over to him asking him to get her husband a record deal and she didn't immediately shove Jackson's tape into his hand. She asked for
advice, clearly appealing to his status and putting herself
in the position of the uninformed novice. This allowed a
natural conversation to develop, during the course of which

she was able to practice good PR by singing her husband's praises.

## The Art of Positive Impressions

Networking can often be the thing that helps move your husband up the ranks. But the higher up he moves, the more you may have to contribute in the way of public relations. Perhaps the clearest example of a wife fostering a positive public persona for her spouse is in the political realm. Few would deny that a large part of John F. Kennedy's appeal was his genteel, lovely wife Jackie. Whatever happened with her husband's approval ratings, the public's admiration for Laura Bush remained consistently high, usually in the 80 percent range. So important is PR among political spouses that during presidential campaigns newspapers frequently poll the public on how they feel about the candidates' spouses as a predictor for which one will win. So perhaps nobody can provide a better example for wives who would learn how to enhance their husbands' public image than a woman whose spouse is on the campaign trail.

The involvement of a wife in her husband's governing role has become controversial in the last two decades, but the one role she is always expected, indeed demanded, to fill is enhancing her husband's public image. When she doesn't, people get suspicious. Take, for example, Howard Dean in the 2004 presidential race. He was an early frontrunner, but several factors contributed to derailing his ambitions. Certainly one of those was the absence of his wife on the campaign trail. Where, pundits continually asked, was she? The implication was that even this man's spouse didn't believe in him enough to campaign for him. Of course Mrs. Dean had every right not to involve herself in campaigning if she didn't want to, but it was clear her low profile hurt her husband's public image. By contrast, early in the 2008 presidential race, one of the significant factors helping relative newcomer Barack Obama break away from the Democratic pack was his wife Michelle's PR skills.

Unlike most wives whose husbands are running for president, Michelle Obama doesn't go up to the podium and expound solely on Obama's good qualities. She recognizes that women are often persuaded to vote for a candidate when they connect with him not just as a politician but also as a person. Michelle Obama responds to this desire by joking that her husband is sometimes a slob who fails to put his socks in the hamper just like theirs. At a campaign stop in Chicago, she joked to the crowd, "Today, he still didn't put the butter up after he made his breakfast. I was like, 'You're just asking for it. You know I'm giving a speech. Why don't you just put the butter up?'"

These faults don't make Obama look like a less-qualified candidate; they make him look charming. Women voters, particularly married women voters, see that for all his elevated position, he is still just like their husbands in many fundamental ways. They then feel that they know Senator Obama and they are more comfortable with him. Of course, once she's made that connection, Michelle Obama immediately turns to paint a brilliant picture of her husband as a potential commander in chief.

Listen to how she explained to *Vanity Fair* how she overcame her initial qualms about her husband's involvement in politics: "I never had a doubt about what Barack could offer, and that's what kind of spiraled me out of my own doubt. I don't want to be the person that holds back a potential answer to the nation's challenges." With this comment, not only does she make Obama look like an accessible leader who's not out for power but for service, she actually turns his short tenure as a public servant into a positive, reinforcing his campaign image of being a new solution to a set of old political problems. It's a one-two punch that leaves his opponents reeling. One of the fundamental lessons of public relations is that you always cast your clients in the best light, extolling their assets and minimizing their shortcomings. But more important than this is authenticity. In conversation about your husband, be genuine first.

That said, sometimes wives can go too far in the other direction—criticizing their husbands in public for the amusement of others. We've all done it, tried to one-up each other with funny tales of our spouse's foibles: *You think your husband's lazy. Mine won't even get off the couch to look for the remote. He'll just keep watching the same station till I come in to find it for him.* A small amount of this can be a bit of good-natured fun and help foster connections (an important component of networking). But consider: if you're constantly cracking jokes about your husband's laziness to your friends, are they or their spouses likely to want to give him a recommendation or let him know about a job opening when it's their reputation on the line? You want to be genuine, but selectively genuine. It's funny when Michelle Obama tells tales of her husband not putting his socks away because it has no bearing on his job performance. We don't question whether he would make a good presidential candidate because of it. If she cracked wise to reporters about how naïve or forgetful he is, that would be a different story.

## Building Goodwill

Public relations can take on a new cast once your husband is in a position of authority. At first glance, it may seem that this is the time when you can stop worrying about enhancing his image with others. But if anything, that is when it becomes more important. It is trickier to stay likable when you are the boss. And while being likable may not be the most important ingredient of a successful career, it can solve a lot of problems before they start.

Part of running a successful business is promoting employee satisfaction and keeping turnover low. Gloria Morgan says that she is far more adept at this work than her husband Frank: "I'm kind of the thermostat for the office. I'm the one that will typically go around to people and sit in their offices for a while, ask how they're doing, ask about their families."

She also heads off potential bad feelings: "Well, sometimes people will tell me I don't know what kind of Frank we're going to get today. He has very sweet moments and can be a real people-pleaser but he can also be quick-tempered. I'm very analytical, so I can dissect a problem with an employee several different ways. It's not like I am going to contradict Frank on something, but I can soften the blow. And I'm really steady, so I'm always doing damage control. Basically I keep everything on an even keel so nobody gets flustered."

As a three-star admiral, Rocky Spane's naval career demanded so much of his wife Linda as well as him that she says they always thought of themselves as a "two-person, one-paycheck team," explaining that "when the spouse of the commanding officer is involved, things just seem to run smoother." The military is in many ways a unique micro-cosm, because "employees" don't have the option of quitting if they suddenly decide they don't like their job or no longer want to work for their boss. But that didn't diminish Linda's role in enhancing goodwill with her husband's charges. If anything, it made her role even more important.

"As you progress in rank," explains Linda, "the number of people that work for your husband gets larger and larger. And we always noticed that when the enlisteds' spouses were not involved with one another socially, the morale of the squadron or ship's company really suffered, making the com-manding officer [CO] look less effective. Because when their spouses at home are lonely, fearful, or unhappy, the company knows about it. So I quickly learned how big an impact I could have by checking in with the wives, making sure they felt they were connected and being taken care of."

Linda found that it didn't take massive formal efforts on her part to maintain goodwill among the naval spouses. It only required her to reach out and do the things that women often naturally do anyway. "Even something as simple as or-ganizing weekly outings to the movies or shopping could do a lot for morale," she remembers. "I tried to make it fun for them. We'd get together once a month and have different kinds of activities like Christmas and Halloween parties, just trying to make it fun for the season. The goal was for the men to know that the women were happy so that they could con-centrate on their mission. And many times, when their hus-band's service was up, the wives would say, 'I can't believe it's over. We had such a good time.' And that felt like a real com-pliment to me, because it really was a job organizing those events and keeping up with everybody."

Though her husband came to appreciate her contribution

later, at the time Linda was working solely from her own initiative. "I don't even know if Rocky was aware of what went
on, because he was deployed so much," states Linda. "He certainly wouldn't have thought to ask me to do it, because most
of it went on without him around. It's when the men are deployed that a close network develops with the women. Certainly those activities were an outlet for us and we looked
forward to being together, but it served a lot of practical purposes too. And I think Rocky would be the first to tell you
that my efforts helped him move up through the ranks." She
was right, he was.

Companies are always in flux. People move up, move
away, move in new directions. Making and maintaining connections helps your husband stay prepared to move as well.
And when you take on public relations and networking tasks
like accompanying him to events that allow the two of you to
become friends and maintain relationships with people connected to his field, over the course of your friendships you
find ways to help one another.

## EXECUTING YOUR GAME PLAN

1. Become more aware of your networking possibilities. List friends, family members, and acquaintances you could be more purposeful about maintaining a relationship with on behalf of your husband. Note how many people you speak to as you go about your daily tasks. Could the man you chat with at the gym have helpful information about your husband's field? Is anyone in your book club connected to his industry?

2. Discuss with close members of your network what you are doing. Explore the possibility of forming a more formal networking group with friends who would be interested in working together.

3. Don't be afraid to reach out to your network for help, especially to other women. We are usually inclined to assist one another any way we can.

4. By the same token, be willing to offer assistance to those who reach out to you.

5. Make yourself more available to opportunities to increase your husband's professional profile. Go to business-related social events. Circulate and introduce yourself to people he works with.

6. Remember that the primary element of public relations is relationship-building. Just be friendly, be yourself, and be open to meeting people.

7. In your conversations, make sure to be genuine but also positive about your husband.

# How Your Skills Can Still Mean Big Bucks Even If You're at Home

When forty-one-year-old Leslie Baird of Parker, Colorado, decided she wanted to be a stay-at-home mom, she assumed it would mean the end of her career producing marketing materials and media projects. She wouldn't work for American Express anymore, so she thought things like video editing, corporate photography, and PowerPoint presentations would be gone from her life forever. Or at least on a hiatus until and if she ever decided to return to work. But then her husband John decided to try for a job in the hugely profitable (and hugely competitive) medical sales industry. If he found one, it would mean a vast improvement in their financial situation, which up to that point had been more than a little tight.

When she first met her husband, Leslie immediately noticed his quirky, outgoing personality, his sharp mind, and his boyish good looks. She also immediately noticed that he didn't appear to be living up to his potential. "I met John when I was in college. He was a little older, out of school, and tending bar at a nice Italian restaurant. And I remember thinking that he was too smart just to tend bar, and"—she laughs—"too old for it too. John was in his late twenties then. After we started seriously dating—by that I mean starting to talk seriously about getting married—the restaurant closed down. Which, from my point of view, turned out to be a really good thing."

It was at that point, when John-the-boyfriend started

thinking about his future as John-the-husband, that he felt a compulsion to find something else to do with his life. He had a degree in communications, but had never during or after college given much thought to how he wanted to apply that degree to a career. Like so many other people, he had simply gone on to a university, because that's what you're supposed to do after high school. Leslie knew this could be a major crossroads for their future and so, along with John, she took stock of his skills and opportunities.

"John's not the type to sit at a desk all day. He really likes being up and around and interacting with people, so he thought he would try sales. He decided to take a job selling copiers door-to-door just to see what he could learn about the business. Three years and lots of awards later we knew he had made the right choice—he really had a knack for it. He won our honeymoon trip to Hawaii in his company's sales contest and everything."

While John now knew he was doing the right thing with his life, however, the position he was in was ground-level, which meant that money was still tight, too tight for Leslie to quit work and stay home with the family they had started. "I loved working during the time that I did," she says. "But our first child was getting older and I wanted to have more, so I definitely felt ready to be a stay-at-home mom." Unfortunately that didn't seem feasible at John's current pay level. ("I was making $18,000 dollars a year at the time," reveals Leslie, "and that was more than him!") Considering their options, John brought up what is widely considered the golden goose of the sales industry: pharmaceuticals.

"We had been talking about it for a long time," Leslie says, "but the field is so competitive—literally hundreds of people apply for every opening. And unless you know someone, or, frankly, are a very good-looking woman, it can be next to impossible to get your foot in the door." Combining that with the fact that his only experience up till then was cold-selling copiers, Leslie didn't think he had much of a shot.

But John applied for an opening anyway, and managed to get to the second interview—the point at which most people end up going no further. "Basically how it works," Leslie explains, "is that they schedule you for that first interview just to size you up—see if you have a nice appearance and to review if you have any experience at all. The second interview is where they really consider you. They give you a pamphlet on one of their products—I think for us it was cough syrup—and you take it home, learn everything you can about it, and come back the next day and try to sell it to the interviewer as if they were a doctor."

When John brought the pamphlet home, Leslie saw an opportunity to do for John what she did at work all day—create a winning presentation that would complement his sales abilities:

*Well, that's what I did at Amex—I made presentations that made people look good for upper management. So I took this little nothing of a pamphlet he brought home, broke it apart, and made a presentation out of it. We made color copies and I retyped in some of the key details, laid it out in what I considered a more compelling fashion, made nice sheets, put it in sleeves, and put it in a nice binder. And then John practiced his sales pitch over and over with me.*

*The next day, he went through the presentation using the visuals we had put together and they realized that he had basically made what is known as a detail aid. And*

*that's what pharmaceutical companies do. They send*
*their reps out to doctors with things like I had made him.*
*They were so impressed, that got him the job. Well, that*
*and his good personality and brains. It amazed them.*
*They had never had anyone do that before.*

From that experience Leslie learned that doing the same
tasks for John that she did for American Express could be the
key to realizing both their ambitions.

In some sense, every chapter in this book is about collaborating. You are working with your husband to help him reach
whatever level of career success he's capable of. But up to this
point we've mostly talked about the psychological support you
can offer him. Helping him identify strengths and pinpoint
how to apply them at work, motivating him to persevere in the
face of obstacles, advising him on day-to-day matters and people problems, and getting out and making connections within
his industry are all important, but they are also somewhat universal. Most wives do them to one degree or another. What
you've learned is how to be more strategic and intentional
about applying them.

Just as valuable, if not more so, however, is offering your
husband help that is unique to you. Of all the characteristics
that the wives of successful men tend to share, none appears
more often or more strongly than their willingness to fill in
the gaps for their husbands' abilities. In virtually every story
I heard, the wife at some point took on duties and performed
tasks that would in any other circumstance have put her on
the payroll. And in fact some of them did end up on it, working with their husbands in an official capacity as partners in
a business. But just as many were women who never saw any
direct rewards from their efforts in the sense that anyone

outside their homes would recognize them. Instead, their recompense was reflected in their spouse's paycheck and performance.

The surface rewards of this type of collaborating are obvious. It can mean a better job, more money, and more prestige. But there are other rewards that are not so apparent. For me, I noticed right away how much closer Brian and I felt to each other when we were both focused on the same goals. Rather than each only half listening to the other because we had separate priorities and, thus, separate conversational tracks running in our heads, we were concentrating on the same subjects. Our discussions were more synergized and more animated. As much as I enjoyed working on this book, one of the drawbacks during that time was that the sense of only half listening to each other (me to him as well as him to me) returned, because he wasn't familiar enough with what I was doing to talk about it easily, and I was frequently too distracted by it to fully engage with him.

Another bonus that could come as a surprise is that you will probably find that the same tasks you do or used to do begrudgingly at work suddenly feel more enjoyable. There is something about doing a job for someone you love rather than someone you work for that lends the entire enterprise more energy. I equate it to mothers who describe how chores they would have previously considered drudgery are gratifying when they are performing them for their own kids. That's not to say changing diapers or washing windows is always pleasant, but it's more pleasant when it's your child and your windows.

The final added benefit you will probably discover is that your husband is far more grateful for your assistance than your boss or colleagues usually are. It's natural for the people you work with to fail to show appreciation for your efforts—you're paid to do those things, it's expected. But not one of the husbands I spoke to or researched acted as if his wife's assistance was simply his due. No matter how high up the corporate ladder they were (and some were about as high as a person can go), they all expressed the deepest respect for their wife's abilities, praised her lavishly, and seemed sincerely touched that she had done so much to help.

## Going Public with Your Intentions

The first step to being your husband's collaborator is letting him know that you want to be of service to him. We're all familiar with the stereotype that men would rather stay lost than pull over and ask for directions. After all these years the cliché still makes women laugh, (1) because it seems so silly to us and (2) because men continue to prove how true it is. Once again, the difference comes down to our competitive versus collaborative mind frames. Women view problems through a collective, we're-all-in-this together lens, so it makes perfect sense for us to ask for help when we need it, knowing we will be happy to give help when someone else needs it. But men's competitive DNA compels them not to show weakness, not to show any hint that they aren't capable of excelling on their own. And as much as they feel this in average situations, they are even more loath to show weakness in front of their wives. As Dr. Weiss noted in Chapter 1, "[men] need their wives to see them as competent because their wives' view of them is so important to their view of themselves," so they won't readily risk their wives' opinion of them by letting on that they might benefit from some assistance. That doesn't mean that your husband won't happily *take* your help. It just means it won't be his instinct to *ask* for it. At least not at first.

But fear of looking weak in front of you is not the only reason your husband isn't likely to ask for your help without a lot of encouragement from you. Many men today are so afraid of coming off boorish or chauvinistic that they hesitate to ask for help even when they know it's well within their wives' abilities to give it. After everything we've been through—after I have spent three years helping him launch a new career and putting together résumé DVDs and researching different aspects of his business—Brian still looks a little sheepish whenever he asks me if I can edit some video or come up with interesting story ideas for a pitch meeting. Contrary to popular opinion, I have not found that men take their wives' efforts for granted. (Well, at least not those efforts related to their work. Efforts related to cooking or laundry are a different matter.) So don't assume that your husband will fully grasp the extent of your desire to assist him unless you explain it to him.

Finally, psychologists have found that men's love for their wives can also play a factor in keeping them from reaching out for help. They don't want to give their wives any cause to worry, so they keep their work concerns to themselves. The key to overcoming all these challenges is making sure your husband understands that you're not offering to help him with your skills because you doubt his ability to succeed or because you fear for your financial future, but because you want to enhance the positive results he's already achieved. I assume by this point in the book you've probably already discussed the career-partnership concept with your husband to some extent. If not, this is a perfect opportunity to do so. Tell him that by offering to supplement his abilities with yours, you simply hope to help him reach goals faster and more easily. Try something along the lines of *"Honey, I've been reading about all these wives who made a big difference in their husbands' careers because they were willing to help them in any way they could. I would love to do this for you. Is there anything you can think of that I could do that would help you in your work?"* He may not come up with something immediately, but it will get him thinking about the subject and plant the seeds for a more productive conversation later on down the road.

If you approach him with a spirit of confidence in his possibilities, your husband is much more likely to open up. It may take a few attempts, especially if the idea is new to him. But once he sees you putting out effort on his behalf (and once you make him aware how many of today's top business leaders got a significant boost from their wives), he's more likely to be enthusiastic about the idea and begin sharing with you areas where he feels you could make the most difference. Then you can begin thinking creatively together about how and where you can contribute.

## Identifying Your Own Strengths

The second step to being your husband's collaborator is doing for yourself what you did for him in Chapter 2—identifying your strengths and skills and pinpointing opportunities to use them. Every wife is going to have a different background, different level of work experience, and different level of education. But no matter what your educational or work history is, you should have the same level of confidence that you have valuable skills to offer. Leslie Baird was able to use her marketing degree and her corporate experience to help land her husband a good job. But once he was there, she was also able to use talents she didn't pick up in college or at the office.

Though his new position as a sales representative for a large drug company immediately meant a bigger salary for John, to make the most of it he had to hit high sales numbers. The problem was, as the low man on the totem pole, he wouldn't receive much money for the corporate gifts that can go a long way in helping a salesperson make connections. Explains Leslie, "Normally what you see is drug reps hosting really nice lunches in the doctors' offices or hospitals. Or they will buy them nice bottles of wine or something on the company dime. But John was given a really small sales budget until he proved himself, and there was just no way he could do that. He had to be really careful with what he spent."

It was Leslie who came up with the idea of using the money to buy the ingredients typical of promotional products and then creating the actual gift herself:

*I've always enjoyed baking, and I have to say I'm pretty good at it. So the first year John and I decided that our best option was to pick his ten best prospects—and put together a basket of cookies for them. I spent days making six different kinds of cookies and brownies, putting them on festive trays, and wrapping them in nice cellophane and ribbon. And I think it did make a difference. I even think some of the doctors preferred it, because it seemed less like the same old cold, corporate bait that way. . . .*

*John's since been promoted to regional sales director, so he doesn't need me to do that anymore, but I still have a picture of him with plates filled with six different kinds of cookies on each one. And it's fun for us to look back on that and see how far we've come.*

When it comes to utilizing your own strengths on behalf of your husband, it's easiest to start with those things that are common solutions to business problems, such as preparing a sales presentation for a job interview. But don't be afraid to approach the situation from a unique angle that still makes use of your gifts. Part of the benefit of not having to give your all to a full-time job is being able to bring a bit of graciousness to your husband's work. Don't underestimate the power of such niceties—Martha Stewart built a billion-dollar business on them.

Of course the lion's share of your collaboration is probably going to come from more traditional business tasks, so you'll want to go back and apply the same techniques in acquainting yourself with your strengths that your husband did with his. Talk to the people around you, and take note of the things friends and family routinely say you're good at. Consider the activities you enjoy spending your leisure time on and investigate whether there isn't some talent there that you could be using to give your husband a boost. If need be, take a strengths-finding tests yourself. And review your own résumé and discuss how the skills you've developed coincide with his work.

MacKenzie Bezos was not only willing to offer her husband Jeff emotional support as he chased his dream of founding Amazon.com, she offered him every kind of tangible support she could as well. She made phone calls, ordered and purchased materials, acted as a secretary, accountant, and researcher—whatever she felt capable of handling. Even if she wasn't yet capable enough to handle it, as in the case of Amazon's bookkeeping needs, she quickly taught herself what she needed to know and was Amazon's accounting department for a year and a half until they finally hired someone for the job. Paul Davis, one of Amazon's first programmers, said of those early days, "We wouldn't have been operational without MacKenzie. She was vitally important."

What prompted MacKenzie Bezos to act as Amazon's gal Friday, picking up the slack wherever she was needed? One, she clearly had a stake in seeing the company grow and become profitable. But she is also known for being strong in areas that require attention to detail. You too have unique strengths, so while helping your husband act on his, remember to identify, exercise, and contribute your own. Whatever ambitions you and your husband hold for his work life, if you are willing to offer him the value of your whole range of abilities, you tip the odds of success dramatically in your favor.

Even if you have the same the strengths as your husband, chances are he could still benefit from them. Obviously Alfred Hitchcock was a more than capable filmmaker on his own, but being able to rely on his wife to edit scripts, analyze scene structure, and participate in story conferences made him that much better. And dozens of bestselling authors, from Mark Twain to Stephen King to *Da Vinci Code* author Dan Brown, have revealed that they relied on their wives for research, editing, and ideas. Interestingly, when doing a piece on individuals who have contributed to the work of their famous author spouses, the *Boston Globe* could not come up with a single man who had done much to further his wife's writing career. Some might argue that's because women are still oppressed by gender stereotypes. But as these kinds of partnerships have continued decade after decade, from John Stuart Mill in the nineteenth century to novelist Richard

Ford in the twenty-first, despite our changing social beliefs, I'm inclined to believe it's because literary wives have found a way to truly have it all. They enjoy the material comforts of their husband's success, the intellectual stimulation of being a part of his work, and the financial freedom to pursue interests they like.

## Compensating for His Weaknesses

Sometimes the opportunity to offer hands-on help won't come so much from what you're good at as what your husband isn't. As we saw in Chapter 2, we all have areas where, no matter how much effort we put in, we aren't going to excel. We also have things that we are so naturally terrible at we have little motivation to bother trying to get better. The best scenario for this situation will be that you are strong in the areas where your husband is weak. And, in fact, this is often the case. But even if you aren't an ace at his area of weakness, if you are better at it than he is and he doesn't have the resources to fill the need in some other way, you may still want to consider doing it for him.

Conventional wisdom has it that people who have risen to the tops of their fields do so because they have learned to overcome their weak points. What isn't commonly known is that the way they most often overcome them is by pooling their resources with another person.

During their study on high achievers, one of the things Donald Clifton and former Gallup executive Marcus Buckingham found was that these achievers didn't worry much about their weak areas. To the extent that they did worry, it was only insofar as these weaknesses interfered with their strengths. If the weak areas didn't interfere—that is, if they didn't keep the executives from applying their strengths effectively—they ignored them. They didn't even consider them weaknesses, just irrelevant skills that they didn't happen to be good at.

Buckingham and Clifton were surprised to find that when it came to shortcomings that *did* have the potential to undermine effectiveness, their excellent performers didn't worry much about those either. But just because they didn't spend much time worrying about them didn't mean that they didn't make sure that *somebody* did. It just didn't happen to be them. Instead, in those instances they mitigated their weaknesses by teaming up with someone who could perform the tasks they weren't suited to.

John Cannistraro Sr., founder of the J. C. Cannistraro Company, is a heavyweight in the world of Boston construction. As the largest privately owned mechanical contractor in New England, the plumbing company boasts a staff of over three hundred and works on massive city and development projects all over the eastern seaboard. One of the most significant factors that boosted Cannistraro to domination in his region was the involvement of his wife, Rita. Though possessed of incredible drive and focus, Cannistraro had little patience for the dropped details that inevitably crop up in a growing company. He had a tendency to let day-to-day hiccups in his plans cause him to get frustrated, and he let certain annoying but necessary tasks like following up on paperwork fall by the wayside.

Rita, on the other hand, didn't mind keeping track of and addressing such issues. Cannistraro recalls how, though she had no background in engineering and no formal job in the company, his wife remained engaged with his daily work, helping out wherever she could: "After we got going, and I bought my first building, I would come home stressed. Rita would ask me questions. She would take notes. Then she'd go into the home office and write a letter, and the problem would go away," he marvels.

Cannistraro remembers a particular instance when he had to make some last-minute changes to an order and was having trouble getting the developer and contractor to sign off on them. He and Rita had stopped by the contractor's office on their way out to dinner, thinking it would only take a few minutes to deal with the errand. Instead, the contractor told Cannistraro they couldn't approve the changes until each issue was filed separately. This could have posed a significant problem for his growing business, costing him money by putting him behind on his work schedule. "So," he says, "Rita asked if she could borrow their typewriter and some paper. She was eight months pregnant, but she sat there, reorganized all the information, and typed everything up. . . . We got it taken care of that night."

Rita Cannistraro knew that her husband's ability to land big contracts and strategize long term could build a great company as long as his low tolerance for taking care of details didn't undermine him. Instead of nagging him not to forget to follow up on small issues, she did it for him, ensuring that his weakness didn't become an obstacle to the goals they were trying to achieve together.

The dangerous aspect of using the strategy of standing in the gaps for your husband is that it involves acknowledging areas where he's lacking. In some cases, like John Cannistraro's, he will hate those chores so much he'll be more than happy if you offer to take them off his hands. In others, though, he may not be aware that he needs help, and sensitivity will be essential.

Addressing the shortcomings that could be holding your husband back is, frankly, a delicate job. Some men will be more open to it than others. That shouldn't keep you from offering to make a contribution where you can, but it's wise to use what I think of as the Emily Dickinson approach to weaknesses—tell the truth, but tell it slant. This means not saying to your husband, "I'm reading this book that says I should take over some of the jobs you stink at so that you don't sabotage yourself." Instead, use a positive approach that helps him envision what he stands to gain by allowing you to fill in for his weak areas.

The good news is that using the collaborating principle to keep your husband's weaknesses from undermining him allows you to neatly sidestep the issue of nagging. My husband, for example, isn't necessarily bad at writing, but he hates doing it. When he first started job-hunting in broadcasting, I would "remind" him often how important it was to tailor his cover letters to each station. "It's Copywriting 101," I would lecture him. "Find out what they want and emphasize the fact that you have it." Yet invariably I saw him sending the same generic form letter I had drafted with every tape. It didn't take me long to figure out that by insisting Brian do it himself—instead of, oh, I don't know, using my skills as a professional writer to do it for him—I was depriving us both of a possibly wonderful opportunity.

## Clearing His Schedule to Maximize His Productivity

On the other hand, there are some tasks your husband could do just fine by himself or could hire someone else to do but that you still might consider doing for him. This is the point at which the hackles of some women will rise, their reaction being, "Well, if he can do it himself, then he should!" I understand this, but I encourage you to take a moment to reorient your thinking.

On the surface this suggestion can smack of subordination, as though you are your husband's underling rather than his equal partner. I sympathize with your fear, but I'm also betting that for most of you it is groundless. Are you really reacting to your husband's personality and behavior, or are you reacting to some mythological beer-swilling Neanderthal that has long haunted the battle of the sexes? I'm not saying these men don't still exist, I'm just saying I don't know any. The men I know and the men I have interviewed and researched appreciate their wives' help and respond by working hard to give them a return on their investment.

I would also remind you that following these strategies is not about being servile, it's about getting results. True, you are doing these things to help your husband, but you are also doing them to help yourself—to give yourself the financial freedom of choosing what kind of life you want to live and how to spend your time. If taking over the bills at home or doing some accounting at his office makes it more likely that you will attain the things you want, are the ghosts of feminism's past really a good enough reason not to?

When thirty-two-year-old Zach Johnson first started playing golf professionally, he was hardly a clear contender for one of the game's highest honors. Like Raja Bell's, his reputation developed slowly, and he admits he wasn't the best on either his high school or his college team. He had strong fundamental skills, but he wasn't yet ready for the Professional Golfers Association. Instead he turned pro by joining the Hooters Tour. But around 2003, a positive change started to occur in Johnson's game. His statistics improved and he qualified for the PGA.

Yet even as his execution steadily improved, he still managed to fly under the press's radar. So when he suddenly, at least to the media's mind, came out of nowhere to defeat Tiger Woods in the 2007 Masters championship, many reporters were left asking, "Who is this guy?" "I'm Zach Johnson," Johnson replied when that exact question was posed to him at a press conference following his unprecedented win, "and I'm as normal as they come."

As the first person outside the top 50 in the Official World Golf Ranking to win the Masters Tournament, Johnson made history, causing many sports reporters to start digging into his theretofore unknown record. What many noted was that his marked improvement seemed to coincide with his marriage to his wife Kim.

Both Kim and Zach concede that she has probably had quite a bit to do with his change of fortune (the Masters win alone grossed him $1.3 million). While both cite her emotional support as a factor (one of the stories to come out of that tournament was how Kim had ordered specialized golf ball markers with a Bible verse that was meaningful to the couple on one side, and the encouraging line she would often say to him, "Trust your Line. One shot at a time," on the other), they also credit the responsibilities Kim has taken off Zach's plate. Many of the tasks seem small, Kim says, but together they can drain a golfer's ability to focus.

"The game demands so much of a person, I say all the time I don't know how the guys who aren't married do it," Kim comments. "So I definitely think the fact that I took over everything else has had an impact." Asked what specific tasks she's referring to, Kim laughs. "Um, everything? I took over the banking and the travel plans and all the extraneous stuff so he really could just focus on the golf." The result of her efforts was that Zach "no longer had to worry. He no longer had to divide his head space between the game and 'Oh, I've got to get this check to the bank or I've got to get that bill paid.' He doesn't have to worry about that stuff anymore because I'm there to take care of it for him."

To take over these roles for her husband and join him on the PGA circuit also required Kim to leave her own job as a social worker, but it's a decision she says she's never regretted: "Most PGA professional wives have had to leave a career to go on the road. We joke that we've left one job only to take on ten. But I'm definitely happier doing what I'm doing now. I mean, I loved my job and I loved working in the social services field, and it was hard for me to leave, because I had spent a lot of time building relationships. But I love what I'm doing now more. I can't imagine not being with Zach every day."

Part of the reason Kim was able to lift so much of the weight off Zach's shoulders was that his job is so individually focused. He doesn't have coworkers in the traditional sense, and his day doesn't involve regular hours, budgets, meetings, or any of the other things your husband probably has to contend with. But no matter what your husband's field is—sales, construction, or even e-commerce—your willingness to lend a hand can have a significant impact on his earning power.

## Helping When He Doesn't Ask

For a variety of reasons—whether he's faced a series of setbacks and is feeling demoralized or he isn't yet used to the idea of a career partnership and doesn't see any opportunity for you to help him—there may be times when you have to take the initiative to help your husband without his involvement.

You don't want to be pushy or impulsive, inserting yourself into areas where it isn't appropriate, but neither do you want to let your husband's emotional state or his inability to understand the idea of a career partnership deter you from getting started. Until he is on board and you can clearly discuss how you are going to use your skills on his behalf, a good rule of thumb to follow is this: If you can help him in a way that isn't public, that doesn't require you to go to his office or speak to his coworkers, and that is reversible, then it's probably safe.

Despite the medical community's pressing need for them, because of the difficulty of the training required, there are only about 120 orthopedic oncologists in the entire United States. Had Craig Cameron's wife Sue not stepped in to help her husband after he had experienced several failures in a row, there would have been one less.

When he first began applying to medical schools, Craig Cameron was an unusual candidate. He had started college late because of turmoil in his family. Then, after a poor performance during his first two semesters, he decided to take time out to join the Air Force, figuring this would help him develop discipline as well as earn some money for his education. In the following years he completed a degree in biology, fell in love, married, and started both a family and graduate school. But in the back of his mind, despite a freshman year that had left him with a less-than-exemplary academic transcript, he still thought of being a surgeon.

Finally, Sue, whose own father had always regretted not pursuing a different career, implored her husband to at least try. She gave him the $5,000 she had inherited from her grandmother to cover the expensive medical school applications. So at twenty-eight years old, now the father of two children, Craig Cameron applied to thirty-three MD programs. He didn't get into any.

At this point, almost everyone advised him it was time to let the goal of being a surgeon go. Even his parents said this was probably a sign that he was supposed to do something else with his life. Only Sue felt differently. "I could see he wasn't ready to give up the dream," she says, "but he wasn't ready to try again. It was like the air had been punched out of him, and he was just deflated. He had worked so hard and for it not to happen . . . he was so disappointed. And everyone he knew was telling him it was the wrong thing."

But the most important person in his life—his wife—didn't believe it was the wrong thing, and she wasn't ready to let go either. She began looking for an alternative route and encouraged her husband to consider doctor of osteopathy programs. This solution would still prove problematic, as most DO graduates go on to be general practitioners, meaning once Craig was finished with school he would face stiff competition from MD program grads for surgical residencies. But without acceptance to an MD program, he had no other option.

At that point Craig was still feeling too beat up to try again. And he didn't want to feel like an irresponsible husband and father by spending more money applying for medical schools when he'd already been turned down by so many. So, to help her husband envision a new possibility for achieving his goal, Sue filled out the first DO application herself and showed it to him. It wasn't his ideal path, but it could still take him where he wanted to go. For the first time since the rejection letters started arriving, her husband seemed hopeful, indicating to Sue that she was doing the right thing.

Yet still Craig didn't move to do anything with the first application she had filled out, let alone submit more. Sue says it finally dawned on her that he was overwhelmed not just from having faced such a huge defeat, but because of his many responsibilities as well. "I knew he didn't have the energy to go to grad school, to work, and to start reapplying," she recalls, so she did it for him.

Using answers and essays she copied from his previous applications, she applied to eleven DO programs. Recalls Sue, "I remember sitting in the backyard with a little electric typewriter while the kids were running around, and I would sit at a card table in the sun and fill out applications." When she was finished with one, she would give it to Craig to look over and sign before taking it to the post office. This time he got into five schools.

Though the road from that point still proved challenging, Dr. Cameron eventually achieved a career he loves in one of medicine's most respected specialties. Asked what he feels his wife's greatest contribution to his success has been, he has trouble choosing, but settles on this: "I always felt like we were doing it all together, that's what she's contributed. We went to medical school together, we did my residency together, my fellowship together—all of it together. I always knew that she was in my corner and that I could count on her to help make my goals, which were really *our* goals, happen."

Even though Dr. Cameron wasn't at first a participant in (or even aware of) his wife's endeavor to find him another route to becoming a surgeon, nothing Sue did could have hurt him professionally. There was no need to involve anyone from his current job or from his grad program in her efforts, and if her husband decided that he wasn't interested in enrolling in a DO program after Sue sent in the first application, they weren't out anything but a little money. Craig could just decline the acceptance.

Collaborating with your husband will probably demand more of you than career coaching, motivating, advising, relating to the public, or networking. It involves much more than conversation and listening. And if you are a mom, adding more responsibilities to your already long to-do list might not sound too appealing. The good news is that in most of these cases, the wives didn't have to take on tasks for their husbands indefinitely.

Leslie Baird no longer has to create her husband's sales presentations or his corporate gifts—he has a staff of people working under him that can do that now. MacKenzie Bezos now spends her days caring for her children and writing novels. Rita Cannistraro's husband John retired several years ago, but his days of needing his wife to act as his secretary were over long before that. Kim Johnson still accompanies her husband on the PGA Tour, but now they drive from hotel to hotel in a decked-out tour bus, and she can afford to hire people to help her with administrative details. And the most help Dr. Cameron asks of his wife these days is that she accompany him to medical conferences in beautiful locations all over the world.

Like most business ventures, a career partnership requires the most heavy lifting on the front end. But the rewards make themselves felt for years to come.

# ENACTING YOUR GAME PLAN

1. Talk to your husband about your desire to help him. Ask him if he sees ways you might be able to help his career, and let him know you're available. Make it clear to him that you are motivated only by your desire to help him capitalize on his talent and opportunities, not by any fear of the future or lack of confidence in him.

2. Take an assessment of your own strengths. What jobs have you held, what was your major in college? What hobbies do you have that require a particular set of skills? Whatever your work or educational history, don't sell yourself short—abilities that seem simple or unimpressive to you could have a major impact on your husband's career.

3. Carefully (oh so carefully) take an assessment of your husband's weaknesses. Are there certain areas where his shortcomings are holding him back? Weigh the feasibility of taking over those tasks for him.

4. Don't wait for your husband to ask for your help or to point out areas where he needs it. Look for opportunities to assist that even he may not be aware of. But be judicious about your efforts—don't take any action that might embarrass him publicly or jeopardize his reputation among his colleagues or that you can't undo if it turns out to be something he doesn't want.

# 7

# Keeping Your Perspective and Enjoying Your Life

It may sound counterintuitive, but for some of you the best way to help your husband achieve more in his work will be to encourage him to devote his time and mental energy to it less. We've developed a sort of work-worship in America these days, forgetting that our jobs are there to service our lives, not our lives to service our jobs. Today's workers put in two hundred more hours on the job than they did in 1973, and a third don't use their vacation time. The advent of cellular and cyber technology is making the problem worse, as there is hardly a moment when we are truly "off the clock." And recent years have even given rise to a phenomenon known as the "extreme worker"—people characterized by seventy-hour-or-more workweeks, constant availability to address work issues, and little downtime.

It doesn't help matters that our culture tends to treat this kind of work addiction as a badge of honor—a sign of integrity—rather than the serious sickness it is. After conducting a study for the Center for Work-Life Policy, economist Sylvia Ann Hewlett found that of the millions of Americans who qualify as extreme workers, 58 percent let the intensity of their jobs and the absence of leisure time interfere with their relationships with their children and spouses. They even allowed it to keep them from maintaining satisfying sex lives. What kind of a life is that? Bleak as Hewlett's report is, it doesn't even begin to touch on well-documented health issues like heart attack, stroke, depression, and even cancer that medical professionals warn overwork can lead to.

But perhaps the worst news about overwork is that many researchers have found that a significant portion of the tasks everyone is running around doing is so much pointless wheelspinning—it can actually be *counterproductive* to success, because people lose perspective and the ability to strategize effectively. In fact, companies in which chronic overwork is an issue are less profitable than those where employees make full use of vacation and personal time. Encouraging workers to have a healthy balance between work and the rest of their life can actually help a business's bottom line.

## Vacationing for Fun and Profit

One of the most fascinating examples of the work-less, make-more concept has to be Google. From its founding, its benefit package has been legendary, offering employees three weeks of paid vacation the first year, almost five weeks the second year, eighteen weeks of paid maternity leave, seven weeks of paid paternity leave, and unlimited sick days. While the old corporate wisdom dictates that a company that allows workers so much time away from their jobs will pay a high price in productivity, Google is instead one of the most profitable, productive enterprises in the world. Why? Google management believes (and apparently with good reason) that their vacation and leave policies promote enthusiasm for their jobs and innovative thinking among employees.

Between Google and conventional business thinking, statistics side with Google. In 2007, using tools originally engineered for astronauts, NASA scientists tested the time off=productivity hypothesis on more typical workers. What they discovered was that after a vacation, employee performance immediately spiked 82 percent before settling into a lasting increase of 25 percent. Another study found that expanding vacation policies to three weeks caused company profits to grow 15 to 50 percent.

A long weekend, however, does not a productivity-increasing vacation make. Research shows that people cannot really reap the benefits of downtime unless they allow themselves significant time to disengage their minds from work. This means that you and your husband need to schedule at least one week, preferably two weeks, of off-the-Internet-and-cellphone-grid vacation a year. As Harvard Medical School psychiatrist Edward Hallowell told *BusinessWeek,* "Making yourself available 24/7 does not create peak performance. Re-creating the boundaries that technology has eroded does."

Our brains and bodies are not inexhaustible machines. They need to time recharge and refocus to avoid burnout. This is especially true given the knowledge-based economy we are now living in, where the greatest financial gains come from creative thinking—something that is impossible to do with a work-fried mind. After conducting an extensive study on the subject of productivity and hours worked, the Families and Work Institute found that "actions by employers to . . . urge and help employees 'get a life' off the job are crucial to improving employee productivity over the long run—not to mention the obvious benefits to workers and their families." If we accept that this is true, it also follows that actions by wives to urge and help their husbands to "get a life" will have the same effect. By helping your husband take time away from the office, you can actually enable him to achieve more when he is there. The problem, of course, is convincing him of this.

## Saying No for Him

Have you ever seen the beer commercials where a group of male celebrities, all famous for exhibiting some exaggerated form of masculinity, are sitting around the table voting on "Man Laws"—rules that all men agree to and that will cost them prestige points in front of the rest of the men if they break them? Sometimes I think there is an actual man law that dictates no man can refuse the call of work no matter what time it comes in, how long it will take, or how intrusive the caller. To say, "I am unavailable for work-related emergencies [which are hardly ever real emergencies] right now" would cause them to break the law and lose face in front of all the other men.

Even requesting time that is officially theirs—their vacation, comp days, and personal days—seems to make men feel guilty. I have actually had to argue Brian into using his comp days before he began a new employment year and lost them. The paradoxical thing about the conflict was that I knew he *wanted* to take some time off, and there was no question that he needed to. But he didn't want to admit it to the people he worked with, as though enjoying a long weekend away with his wife were something to be ashamed of.

Because so much of men's identity is tied up in their jobs, they can feel embarrassed about acknowledging they need a break from them. It has gotten so bad that companies like PriceWaterhouseCoopers have instituted mandatory vacation policies, sending out e-mails to employees and their supervisors to remind them how many vacation days they have left to use. Major metropolitan hotels have created "unplugged" packages, where guests are required to surrender their BlackBerrys and laptops to the front desk's vault before beginning their stay. (They report that many such guests emotionally thank them for the transformative experience.) It is at these times that it is necessary for wives to step in and lift the mantle of shame from their husbands by demanding they find time to relax and recharge for their own good. As we have seen, one of the best ways to do this is to appeal to your husband's sense of logic rather than his emotions. He may clearly *feel* exhausted, but that won't necessarily be enough to persuade him to schedule that week in Bermuda. But confronting him with the hard facts I've armed you with above, and the greater performance he stands to lose by not taking regular breaks, will. If that doesn't work, many wives have found that a good old-fashioned bout of "putting their foot down" works pretty well too.

Though he admits he has always had workaholic tendencies, John Cannistraro says that in truth he appreciates his wife's insistence that he take care of himself mentally, physically, and emotionally by scheduling downtime. But in some instances, Rita Cannistraro has had to go beyond laying down the law with her husband; she has had to lay it down with the people he works with.

"What's funny is that when *you* say you won't be available, people don't hear that. They call anyway," reflects John. "I remember one day I was at home, and a call came in. It was quarter to seven, so right in the middle of dinnertime. And this was a guy I had told several times before that I didn't take calls in the evening. I don't remember what the problem was—nothing truly urgent—but I started talking to the guy about it anyway. After a few minutes Rita walked over, took the phone away from me, and said [into the receiver], 'The office is closed.' The guy says, 'But he's right there, this will just take another minute.' Rita just says, 'Please call tomorrow. The office is closed.' She hung up, and we had dinner. And I loved her for that. Whatever it was, it wasn't as important to her as making sure that we got time together and that I got time with my kids."

If a true emergency call comes in, your husband will let you know. But in a work culture where everyone wants a piece of him at all times, one of the most valuable services you can render is acting as a safeguarder for his free time. This will especially be true as his level of professional achievement increases.

Once Zach Johnson won one of golf's highest honors Kim Johnson found that she was suddenly required to play a new part for her husband—that of gatekeeper. Immediately following the Masters Tournament, Johnson was inundated with media requests (one of which, I admit, was my own). Some, like going on the *Today* show and David Letterman, were good for his career; others involved projects he personally believed in. Many were neither.

At first Zach tried to accommodate everyone, but Kim quickly realized that his desire to play the good guy and grant an interview to everyone who asked for it was going to exhaust him and hurt his golf game. Seeing a need, she stepped in.

"I think my role in that is to help him say no. I'm sort of the balancing act that goes 'I think you're overcommitting yourself; I think that's too much,'" she says. "I don't know if I'm the angel or the devil, but I'm definitely on his shoulder in one of his ears telling him he can't let all this attention and the expectations of the press get in the way of our life." Kim Johnson goes on to point out that time away from golf is part of what has helped her husband excel at the game in the last few years:

*I think it's important, especially in golf, because it's such a mental game and it can play with your head so much, to have a life outside of it. It's extremely important to be able to come off the golf course and do things that have nothing to do with golf—to be able to go to a movie or out to dinner and realize there's more to life than what happens on the course. Because I see so many guys obsess on it. They go to their hotel rooms, relive their day, and think about every shot. And that's just not productive. If Zach gives himself too much time to overanalyze everything, he will get in his own way. So that's an important role that I play—I give him a way to get away from it all, and I remind him that at the end of the day it's just a job.*

## Reminding Him He Is More Than His Job

The other important aspect of insisting that your husband have a personal life is that it helps ensure you will never have to live with an egotistical jerk. It reminds him who he is away from his job—that he has an identity beyond lawyer, vice president, weatherman, or whatever his title is.

Forty-eight-year-old Jerry Miller of Newport News, Virginia, is used to getting his way in most situations. After founding his ship-repair company, Earl Industries, in 1984, he grew it into one of the United States Navy's premier servicing firms. This kind of achievement commands a great deal of respect within his field, but as Jerry is the first to confess, such high levels of responsibility can distort a man's perspective on himself.

"I'm at work all day, and if I want something done at work, it happens," he admits. "Sometimes I don't even have to ask for things, because people want to please me and make sure that everything goes right for me because I'm the boss." But at home with his wife and three children, says Jerry, "reality is quite different." And it is that reality that forces him to maintain a healthy perspective on his place in the world. When he's at home, he's with "four people who are a lot more equal than [everyone is] at work. And every so often my wife will have to remind me, 'I'm not one of your employees.' Of course she's right, and I have to apologize for my tone. But I think that's good for me. It's good to be just one of the four people at home who happen to live there. I don't know who I would become if I didn't have that reminder that I'm not the boss everywhere I go," he chuckles.

## Developing a Positive Mind Frame Through Volunteering

Such reminders are important as more than just ego-checks. Spending time with his family can help your husband keep his perspective on more than just himself, it can also help him keep his perspective on what's important. "I do try to give Zach spiritual encouragement that our success isn't necessarily based on how he performs on the golf course but how he lives his life," says Kim Johnson. She believes that her ability to "take some of the pressure off" Zach in this way actually improves performance: "At the end of the day, he knows that it doesn't matter how he plays, he's going to be loved and supported regardless."

As we have seen, positive people experience much more success in business—and, indeed, in life—than negative people. While the tools we discussed in Chapter 3 can be extremely effective in helping your husband develop a more positive outlook on his career, helping him develop a positive outlook on his life requires he feed his mind, soul, and heart with something more than work. I have met many workaholics in my life, and not only are they rarely happy, they rarely contribute to the happiness of the people around them. But there is one almost surefire method of increasing your husband's happiness threshold.

Ask people who donate money and volunteer time to charity why they do it, and at first most will describe the importance of the cause and how it helps the community. But keep prodding and they will usually also reveal that they do it because it makes them feel good. This answer is not just some Pollyanna, hands-across-America bit of pabulum, it is a scientific fact. Studies have found that volunteering causes the brain to release endorphins—the same feel-good chemicals that exercise releases. They have also discovered that it strengthens the immune system, meaning that people who give their time, talent, and money to causes that are important to them experience less sickness than others and even live longer. They also report greater life satisfaction in general.

Participating in causes that are meaningful to him can also bring a greater sense of honor to your husband's work. It reminds you both that the purpose of striving for financial success is not just to improve your own lives, but to improve the lives of others as well. Author and Benedictine nun Joan Chittister has said of the spiritual side of work, "We do not work for ourselves, we work so that others may not want. We work for the gain for the next generation. Work involves us in the exercise of world-building, of co-creation, and we must each of us, in each age, work in new ways to achieve it." In so saying, Chittister also brings up the point that acknowledging the spiritual side of work gives it more meaning. Giving it greater meaning makes it more fulfilling.

When work is more fulfilling, we tend to be more successful at it.

Professional achievement is not the be-all and end-all of a successful, satisfying life. What is the point of helping your husband reach all this success if you never take the time to enjoy it together? How beneficial is wealth, really, if it turns your husband into a self-centered, stressed-out grouch who is unable to enjoy other, more important parts of his life? Whether it's making sure they feed their spiritual sides, participate in organizations that better their communities, or just relax and enjoy stress-free time with their families, the wives of successful men help their husbands keep their focus on the bigger picture.

## ENACTING YOUR GAME PLAN

1. If your husband is unable to ignore the call of the office (and he feels it is appropriate), say no for him. His coworkers are actually more likely to respect a no that comes from you than one from him.

2. If possible, schedule off-grid hours—times when no one in the family is available by phone, e-mail, or pager.

3. Remind him who he is away from work by scheduling time together with your family where his job is not the focus.

4. Choose causes and activities that give the work you and your husband are doing together a deeper purpose. Remember that the efforts he is putting in and the efforts you are putting in with him can benefit not only your own family but your community as well.

## CONCLUSION

# More Than Just a Married Woman

The Japanese have a proverb that says, "Every married woman is not a wife." It also follows, then, that not every married man is a husband. So what is it that takes people from generic spouses who happen to be married to true husbands and wives? Obviously love is a major part of that equation. But I believe the other defining element is partnership, the interdependence that occurs through recognizing and serving each other's needs, aspirations, and desires. It's what makes two people more than individuals who happen to share homes and bodies. It makes them a new, separate thing—a single unit.

Unfortunately, I also believe that in the last few decades the value of marital interdependence has been undermined somewhat. Though the feminist movement was essential and positive in many respects, certain factions of it have led us to a place where women are encouraged to treat their husbands as rivals and their homes as battlegrounds over whether everyone is doing the same amount of the dishes and earning. Those of us born after 1970, in particular, were taught that the only way to be a person of significance and to have a worthwhile life was to follow the male model of achievement. We were admonished to behave more like men and they to behave more like us. Never mind whether one party preferred certain responsibilities more than the other. We were each to be independent coresidents in our households. And the thing that makes us husbands and wives—our ability to rely on each other and our willingness to help each other become the people we want to be and create the lives we want to live—got lost in the shuffle.

But the women I investigated for this book were different. Their behavior was different, their outlooks on life and marriage were different, and their relationships were different. Yes, they used their time and talents to help further their husbands' goals, but this didn't make them second-string players in their own lives. If anything, from their husbands' point of view, they were coaches. They may not have been the ones on the field, but by helping their husbands formulate and carry out plans for career success, they were furthering their own goals as well. And like those of coaches, their influence and contributions were wide-ranging. Wherever they saw a weak spot, they sought to shore it up. Their husbands, in turn, were serving more than their own ambitions in striving for greater levels of professional achievement. They were serving their families and expressing their love for their wives by trying to bring home a win for the team.

In the interest of space, with most of the women referenced in this book, I had to choose only one principle to focus on. But in almost all the cases, the women exhibited all of the principles. Joan Weill not only advised her husband, when he first started out on Wall Street and couldn't get anyone besides his mother to invest with him, she also networked and called on old friends (and even old boyfriends!) to help build his client list. When his shy, introverted nature threatened to sideline his leadership potential, she employed her own bubbly personality to raise his profile on the New York social scene. And when the partner he'd leaned on heavily for direction when his firm was still small suddenly abandoned him, she motivated him with encouraging words, assuring him that he possessed the necessary skills to assume control and carry the company to even greater success.

You saw how Richard Parsons's wife Laura helped him pinpoint his strengths and apply them to his career, but what you didn't see was that she also motivated him with her positive encouragement, and insisted he find activities, like maintaining a winery, that offered him stress release outside of work.

While it's true that Alma Hitchcock was her husband's closest adviser on his films, she was also known to roll up her sleeves to help write scripts, edit tape, and audition actors. When it came to making connections on his behalf, she was a consummate public relator and networker, regularly planning and hosting elaborate meals and weekend getaways with other important film industry figures. And Gloria Morgan not only motivated her husband through the most challenging time in his life—battling cancer and losing his job at the same time—she used her skills to keep the family company running when her husband was at his weakest.

As I mentioned in the prologue, of all the partner-wives I profiled, the strongest model that I look to for guidance is Abigail Adams, wife of our second president, John Adams. Her strength, confidence, intelligence, and eloquence were nearly as significant to her husband's success as his own were. But even more inspiring to me than what their interdependence accomplished politically is the deep affection and admiration that grew out of it. Adams so clearly valued his wife's insight and cherished her companionship that there could be no question of her being anyone's lackey. She truly managed to have it all—all being everything she wanted. She had years at home taking care of her children, she had the excitement of traveling the world and meeting fascinating people, she had the satisfaction of being married to one of the most renowned men of his time, and eventually she had the respect of the world for the impact she had on the nation in her own right. And there isn't a principle in this book that she wasn't adept at and didn't undertake on a regular basis.

For those who aren't familiar with the history of John and Abigail Adams, theirs was not just a powerful political story, but an enduring love story as well. So closely intertwined were their goals and activities that one biographer was compelled to note that they eventually grew to become "almost one soul in two bodies." The seeds for both the love and the success story were planted at the very beginning of their marriage.

Adams lore has it that when the upper-crust Abigail Smith married the son of country farmer John, her parents were less than thrilled. But Abigail saw in her sweetheart the building blocks of a born leader—a sharp mind, a diligent work ethic, and a passionate dedication to his ideals. For John's part, historian David McCullough writes, "[Abigail] was in all respects his equal and the part she was to play would be greater than he could possibly have imagined."

Though Abigail was ambitious for John and eager to help him make the most of his talents, her motivation didn't spring solely out of her love for him. It also sprang out of love for her country. Revolution marked their union from the outset, and it wasn't long before the young bride had to confront the fact that seeing her convictions realized on the world stage would require great risks on her part as well as her husband's. Toward the end of their first year of marriage, John approached his wife (who had just become a new mother) with the news that he had been elected to the Mas-

sachusetts state legislature, a prospect that would mean considerable time away from both home and his burgeoning law
practice. Because it also meant a considerable decrease in his
income, he left the decision of whether to accept the opportunity up to Abigail. Her first reaction was to burst into tears,
but after this initial trepidation subsided, she acted as career
counselor and told him to go: "You cannot be, I know, nor do
I wish to see you, an inactive spectator. We have too many
high-sounding words and too few actions that correspond to
them." She also assured him that she was "very willing to
share in all that was to come."

For most couples, the first major test of how the career-
partnership arrangement is going to play out is something
like deciding whether to quit a job or invest in going back to
school. For the Adamses, it was war, a prospect that took John
even further away from Abigail, as he was then elected to
serve in the Continental Congress in Philadelphia.

Preparing to take a public stand against reconciliation
with England, John looked to his wife as a sounding board
and an encourager. "I want to hear you think . . . to see your
thoughts. . . . I think you shine as a stateswoman," he told her.
Writing to her husband in May 1776, a mere two months before he and fifty-four other men would sign the piece of
paper that could easily have become their death warrants,
Abigail shored him up against any doubts he may have had.
Assuring him that the risk he (and, by extension, she) was
running was worthwhile, she reminded him of the principles
they both fervently believed in. "A Government of more Sta-
bility is much wanted in this colony, and they are ready to receive it from the Hands of the Congress, and since I have
begun with Maxims of State I will add another, that a people
may let a king fall, yet still remain a people, but if a king let

his people slip from him, he is no longer a king. And as this is most certainly our case, why not proclaim to the World in decisive terms our own importance?"

Despite the fact that Abigail had no formal education, John couldn't help but be impressed, as was almost everyone else who knew her, by her deep understanding of political events and the insightful advice she was able to offer because of it. Once the war did come, he even assessed the weaknesses of his foes on the basis of their wives, measuring them up against his own and finding them lacking: "I believe the two Howes [British generals] have not very great women for wives," he wrote to Abigail. "A smart wife would have put Howe in possession of Philadelphia a long time ago."

After independence was won and John's role as a public figure grew, his need for Abigail's assistance only increased. When he traveled to Europe to act first as the United States commissioner to France then as a negotiator to the Paris peace treaty that officially ended the war, it was Abigail who kept him apprised of political developments at home. ("You apologize for the length of your letters," John wrote to his wife, "[but] there are more good thoughts, fine strokes, and mother wit in them than I hear all week.") At home Abigail had to marshal all her business acumen in running the family farm and managing their finances, a task she proved more than adept at. In fact, Adams often joked to neighbors that the farm ran better when he was away.

But the long separations were hard on the Adamses, prompting them to send numerous affectionate, teasing, and sometimes fiery letters to each other. To combat the fear and loneliness that plagued her daily, Abigail consoled herself with the hopeful thought that "I know America capable of anything she undertakes with spirit and vigor." And she motivated John by reminding him that his work was as important to her as it was to him. "My whole soul is absorbed in the idea," she wrote him. "The honor of my dearest friend, the welfare and happiness of this wide, extended country, ages yet unknown, depend for their happiness and security upon the able and skillful, the honest and upright discharge of the important trust committed to you."

In England, John had to contend not only with loneliness and a crushing level of responsibility (bringing an end to the war was riding primarily on his shoulders, after all) but also the ridicule of the British press. They called him a nobody, insulted his weight and his clothes, and sneered at the simple manner of living his income demanded in an expensive city like London. "A man must be a rock to stand it all," her friend Thomas Jefferson wrote to Abigail, admitting that Adams had been a much better choice to carry out the task than he would have been, in part because of her. "I am fond of quiet, willing to do my duty, but made irritable by slander and apt to be forced by it to abandon my post," he confided. "These are weaknesses from which your counsels will preserve Mr. Adams."

Finally, when their isolation from each other grew too much, Abigail agreed to travel across the sea (her greatest fear) to be with her husband. On arrival, she immediately launched a public relations campaign, hosting dinners and attending state events and other gatherings that would improve John's European reputation, a pattern she continued to follow after they returned to the States. During his tenures as vice president and later president, she kept an arduous networking schedule, entertaining guests and visiting both political supporters and detractors on his behalf.

Like those of the twenty-first-century men in this book

who spoke so highly of their wives' contributions, John's reaction was not to take his wife for granted or to expect her assistance as his manly right. Instead, he showed profound gratitude and respect for her abilities. After ascending to the office of the presidency, then headquartered in Philadelphia, he found himself overwhelmed by the demands of a young nation and the backbiting, scheming nature of politics. Though Abigail continued to assure him that he was up to the job, she never minimized the magnitude of the job itself: "You know what is before you, the whips and scorpions, the Thorns without Roses, the dangers, anxieties and weight of an Empire." But she also told him that the presidency would be a "glorious reward" for the sacrifices he had made and that his ability to "discharge [your duties] with honor to yourself, with justice and impartiality to your country, and with the satisfaction to this great people, shall be the daily prayer of your A.A."

Heartening as her letters were, without her physical presence John felt himself crumbling under the weight of the office. And the slanders and accusations being hurled at him by his critics in the press began to eat away at his confidence. Desperate, he begged Abigail to leave their farm, where she had been ill, and come to his side: "I must entreat you not to lose a moment's time in preparing to come, that you may take off from me every care of life but that of my public duty, assist me with your councils, and console me with your conversation. . . . The times are critical and dangerous and I must have you here to assist me. I must now repeat this with zeal and earnestness. I can do nothing without you."

Come she did, and her first order of business was working to offset the damage done by John's rivals. She wrote to friends praising his policies and encouraging them to write to the newspapers on his behalf. And she warned her husband to be on guard against Alexander Hamilton, the man who, though in the same party, would eventually help bring an end to John's political career at the age of sixty-five. ("Beware that spare Cassius [the Roman general who conspired against Julius Caesar] has always occurred to me when I have seen that cock sparrow. I have read his heart in his wicked eyes; the very devil is in them. They are lasciviousness itself," she assessed.)

Having lost his first election after a lifetime of successes, John retired with his wife to their farm in Braintree, Massachusetts. The defeat contained many blessings for Abigail, allowing her to enjoy the rest of their years together knowing that she had fully realized what she had once told John was her fondest dream: "All my desires and all my ambition is to be esteemed and loved by my partner, to join with him in the instruction and education of our little ones, and to set under our own vines in peace, liberty, and safety." Perhaps she still could have realized this dream without supporting her husband in taking a step back in salary to take a step forward as a statesman, had she not motivated him to persevere during the most frightening times, had she not advised him about developments at home and whom he needed to be wary of, had she not constantly worked to form social relationships within his political sphere, had she not taken over responsibilities on the farm, and had she not helped him realize that the work he was doing served far more than his own ambitions. But then again, perhaps not.

The greatest results of Abigail Adams's commitment to partnering with her husband are written all over the pages of history. But I like to think that the happiest result, the one that meant the most to her, were written in the letters from a husband who clearly adored her and whom she loved equally in return. John called Abigail his "best, dearest, worthiest, wisest friend in this world" and confessed that if he were ever to tell her "all the tenderness of my heart, I should do nothing but write you." Reflecting back on their courtship, she told him that the passing years only brought her a deeper attachment to him: "I look back to the early days of our acquaintance and friendship as to the days of love and innocence, and, with an indescribable pleasure, I have seen a score of years roll over our heads with an affection heightened and improved by time, nor have the dreary years of absence in the smallest degree effaced from my mind the image of the dear untitled man to whom I gave my heart."

Researching the Adamses' profound connection to each other, forged through a lifetime of working toward the same goals, Pulitzer Prize–winning biographer David McCullough was prompted to note à la Antoine de Saint-Exupéry, "Real love isn't just gazing into each other's eyes. It's looking out together in the same direction. And if ever there was a man and woman who were truly in love and truly looking out in the same direction, it was John and Abigail Adams."

Could anyone making an honest assessment of her life claim that Abigail Adams was somehow diminished by choosing to invest herself in her husband's career? Could anyone claim that she enjoyed her life any less, that it was any less significant than if she had taken the attitude typical today that her husband's job was his own problem and that she had her own priorities to deal with? It seems most likely that the world would have been deprived of both her influence and John's influence had she done that. His abilities wouldn't have been magnified through their association with hers, and neither would have achieved the same level of greatness.

And this, finally, is the difference between being a married woman and a wife, as well as the difference between being a married man and a husband. Dedication to supporting the other's interests increases not only our effectiveness as individuals—whether it's effectiveness as a parent, a professional, or a spouse—but also our importance to each other. My ambition as of this writing—an ambition that was surely supported and magnified through the involvement of my husband—is not only that this book helped both you and your spouse move closer to realizing your personal and professional goals, but that following its principles moved you closer to each other as well. That it made you more indispensable to each other. That it made you more husband and more wife.

# RESOURCE GUIDE

In helping your husband get ahead at work, you will also need all the help you can get. The following are some wonderful resources I and others have used that offer you chapter-by-chapter support as you carry out the principles of *Beside Every Successful Man.* If you're ever at a loss for how to help your husband with a particular problem, or if you need fresh inspiration for ways to partner with him in his work, the books, research, and websites below will arm you with both information and ideas.

## CHAPTER 2
## HOW TAKING A STEP BACK CAN MOVE YOUR HUSBAND CLOSER TO THE TOP AND YOU CLOSER TO HOME

### Understanding and Applying Strengths

The first step we covered in this chapter was helping your husband isolate and apply his strengths. If you're running into a wall on this point, one of the best tools available is the Gallup Organization's book, *StrengthsFinder 2.0.*

A more conventional, corporate means of strengths-finding

than some of the methods I outlined, it can still get you more acquainted with the strengths mind-frame and help your husband pinpoint his top five strengths. (Just keep in mind, as in the case of Dr. MacMannis and his songwriting, it won't necessarily identify more unique ways your husband could use his talents). As a bonus, it comes with hundreds of ideas for applying strengths at work. It also includes a code for entering a companion web site (www.strengthsfinder.com) where you can access more strengths-finding tools and discussion boards.

*StrengthsFinder 2.0: A New and Upgraded Edition of the On-line Test from Gallup's Now, Discover Your Strengths* by Tom Rath (Gallup Press, 2007). Visit the companion website: www .strengthsfinder.com.

## Risk Assessment and Career Planning

The second step in this chapter involved taking an honest assessment of the risks your family faces if your husband needs to change fields, change jobs, or change locations. As I said, you don't want to analyze this major life decision out of fear, but neither do you want to jump haphazardly into the deep end of the pool.

A career action plan provides a comprehensive method of risk assessment that can help you and your husband map out a clear, structured strategy for a career change. Though often geared for college students, the popular web site About.com has published a concise, easy-to-follow article on developing a career action plan that is appropriate for adults with any level of work experience. It even includes a sample worksheet that can help you and your husband navigate obstacles like finances and elderly parent care.

"Writing a Career Action Plan" by Dawn Rosenberg McKay (About.com). http://careerplanning.about.com/od/careeraction plan/a/action_plan_lng.htm.

## Chapter 3
# MOTIVATING YOUR OTHER HALF: TURNING APPLAUSE INTO PROFIT

### Confronting Worry

One of the first challenges we encountered with being your husband's motivator is women's greater predisposition for chronic worrying. Unless you motivate from a place of confidence yourself, what you intend to be motivating could come out sounding like nagging to your husband.

If you are someone who overthinks to the point of "getting caught in torrents of negative thoughts and emotions" consider picking up *Women Who Think Too Much: How to Break Free of Overthinking and Reclaim Your Life* by Susan Nolen-Hoeksema. Dr. Nolen-Hoeksema provides a practical, straightforward, and extremely well-researched guide to overcoming destructive rumination. No touchy-feely New Age advice here.

*Women Who Think Too Much: How to Break Free of Overthinking and Reclaim Your Life* by Susan Nolen-Hoeksema (Holt Paperbacks, 2004).

### Positive Explanations and Process-Based Visualization

Using effective positive-thinking techniques requires more practiced and concentrated efforts than many motivational gurus suggest. If you need additional guidance on how to incorporate positive explanation and process-based visualization into your interactions with your husband, there's no one better to turn to than the father of positive psychology, Dr. Martin Seligman.

*Learned Optimism: How to Change Your Mind and Your Life* by Martin E. Seligman, Ph.D. (Vintage, 2006). Dr. Seligman's website through the University of Pennsylvania also includes numerous free resources for using the tools of positive psychology: www.authentichappiness.com.

## Chapter 4
## YOUR SECRET SUPERPOWER: HELP ONLY YOU CAN OFFER

### Developing Confidence in your Ability to Advise

As we saw, advising your husband—particularly on matters that relate to personalities and emotions—will probably be a somewhat intuitive process for you. But some of you may still doubt that you're qualified to offer input into your husband's work.

If that's the case, I can't urge you strongly enough to check out Louann Brizendine's work on the female brain. She may be a brilliant neurobiologist with an intimidating list of scholarly credits, but her writing is anything but scholarly and intimidating. With fun stories and clear explanations of the biology of a woman's mind, she outlines why we are so good at reading and responding to people. As a bonus, you'll feel a bit like Wonder Woman once you discover all the unique and amazing talents your female brain is designed for.

*The Female Brain* by Louann Brizendine, M.D. (Broadway, 2006).

## How to Talk So He Will Hear

What won't be so necessarily intuitive is offering your advice in language that makes your husband receptive to it. Perhaps the foremost expert in the world on the subject of gender and communication, linguistics professor Deborah Tannen can help those of you who are having trouble presenting your advice in a persuasive manner to your men. Her tips for making yourself clear with the opposite sex have been tested and proven effective on countless occasions in the Basham household.

*You Just Don't Understand: Men and Women in Conversation* by Deborah Tannen (Harper Paperbacks, 2001).

## CHAPTER 5
## USING YOUR PR SAVVY TO INCREASE HOUSEHOLD CASH FLOW

## Networking and Public Relations

Obviously, many of the traditional business books on public relations and networking won't apply to women working through *Beside Every Successful Man*. Most of you aren't going to have to write press releases trumpeting your husband's achievements (though I wouldn't rule it out, either!) or exchange a set number of business cards at a conference. But that doesn't mean that there isn't something to be gained from these resources. Their corporate-oriented examples may not apply to you, but the tips and suggestions they offer for improving your networking and PR skills will.

*Never Eat Alone: And Other Secrets to Success, One Relationship at a Time* by Keith Ferrazzi (Doubleday Business, 2005).

*The Fine Art of Small Talk: How To Start a Conversation, Keep It Going, Build Networking Skills—and Leave a Positive Impression!* by Deborah Fine (Hyperion, 2005).

### CHAPTER 6
## HOW YOUR SKILLS CAN STILL MEAN BIG BUCKS EVEN IF YOU'RE AT HOME

If you're ever flummoxed on how to use your talents and skills to help give your husband a hand at the workplace, go through the same strengths-finding exercises he is. It may even be fun to take Gallup Organization's strengths tests together to compare where you differ and where your strengths can complement each other.

### CHAPTER 7
## KEEPING YOUR PERSPECTIVE AND ENJOYING YOUR LIFE

### Convincing Your Husband to Give Himself a Break

The first resource you may need to help you with this principle is something to convince your husband he needs to take time off. The following are two serious-minded works that present rock-solid evidence that a vacation now and then *is* worth his time. Even the most business-minded man can't argue with *BusinessWeek,* can he?

"Do Us a Favor, Take a Vacation" (*BusinessWeek,* May 21, 2007). http://www.businessweek.com/magazine/content/07_21/b4035088.htm.

*The Importance of Being Lazy: In Praise of Play, Leisure, and Vacations* by Al Gini (Routledge, 2006).

### Desperate Measures

If you absolutely cannot get your hardworking husband to willingly disconnect from the office, consider booking an off-the-grid hotel stay. Sheraton Chicago Hotel & Towers runs a BlackBerry Check-In program where guests are forced to relinquish the addictive little devices to the front desk until they check out. And the Four Seasons in Silicon Valley occasionally offers an off-the-grid wellness package, reminding potential guests on their website that "you have to unplug before you recharge."

www.fourseasons.com/siliconvalley
www.sheratonchicago.com

## RELATED READING

I'd also like to recommend some additional resources that didn't entirely fit into the purview of this book, yet present information that is very much related. The studies and statistics cited within the pages of *Beside Every Successful Man* only scratched the surface of the research I reviewed. Unfortunately, a lot of it makes for pretty dense reading. But the following books and articles are no such thing. I've only included the best of the best, and they're sure to fascinate and inspire anyone wanting to help her husband get ahead in his work. They will also give those of you who would like to go deeper with the foundational research of this book a place to begin doing so.

## On the Financial Stability of Single-Income Households

Those with a political interest in seeing all women working full-time hours often fall back on the suggestion that families that rely primarily on one paycheck are more vulnerable to money problems than families that rely equally on two.

Harvard Law School professor and bankruptcy expert Elizabeth Warren and her daughter, healthcare specialist Amelia Warren Tyagi, give a startling wake-up call to anyone who believes two-family incomes are any kind of protection against financial disaster. In fact, as the authors prove with a combination of statistics and heartbreaking personal stories, families in which both parents work are 27 percent *more likely* to face bankruptcy than single-earner families.

Warren and Tyagi do not consider such issues as the marriage premium when laying out the picture of family economics in modern America, but they do offer (even if it wasn't their primary intention) compelling evidence that having one spouse forgo a full-time income could help some families avoid financial disasters like foreclosure, bad credit, and bankruptcy.

*The Two-Income Trap: Why Middle Class Mothers and Fathers Are Going Broke* by **Elizabeth Warren** and **Amelia Warren Tyagi** (Basic Books, 2003).

## On Women and Divorce

Much has been made in the media about the dangers of opting out. In fact feminist writer Leslie Bennetts authored an entire book warning women never to take a break from work or even to cut back to part-time hours because their husbands might be permanently injured, or they might die, or leave them. On the dying and injured part, well, one can always look into life and long-term care insurance. On the being left part, Bennetts bases her argument solely on anecdotal evidence and doesn't bother to mention that in fact it is *wives* who do most of the leaving (in the United States women initiate 75 percent of all divorces). Hard statistics, on the other hand, indicate that marriages in which a husband earns more than his wife are significantly less likely to end in divorce than those in which a wife earns as much or more. In the 1990s, for example, stay-at-home wives were 40 percent less likely to get divorced than their working counterparts. The greater the number of hours a wife works also appears to increase the likelihood of divorce.

Not many journal articles about spousal earnings and their impact on divorce statistics pass the layman's test (i.e., few are likely to hold the interest of anyone not working in the fields of sociology or economics, or not writing a relevant book on the subject). But of the many peer-reviewed journal articles demonstrating that a marriage in which a wife earns, or works, more is more likely to end in divorce, the following are two I found especially engaging. You scholarly types might want to give them a look at your local library.

**"The Impact of Husbands' and Wives' Relative Earnings on Marital Disruption" by D. Alex Heckert, Thomas C. Nowak and Kay A. Snyder. (*Journal of Marriage and the Family*, 1998, volume 60, number 3).***

*The only statistically significant results this study reported were that "nontraditional couples [those in which the wife earns 50 to 75 percent of the household income] are more likely to divorce or separate than other couples . . . the odds that these couples will have a marital disruption in a given year are 2.02 times as large as they are for traditional couples."

**"Do Long Work Hours Contribute to Divorce?" by John Johnson (*Topics in Economic Analysis & Policy*, 2004, volume 4, issue 1).***

*What did economics professor Johnson uncover with his study? "First, the incidence of divorce is much greater when both spouses are working than when only one spouse is employed. Second, the work hours of women are more highly correlated with divorce than are the work hours of men."

Some additional perspectives about the issue of women's earnings and divorce that I cited in the Introduction come courtesy of *New York* magazine. The picture they paint is stark and troubling.

**"Alpha Women, Beta Men" by Ralph Gardner Jr. (*New York* magazine, November 2003).**

And finally, not to toot my own horn, but for those who would like to take a short, comprehensive look at why helping your husband succeed won't cause him to abandon you, I encourage you to read an article I wrote for Townhall.com in 2007.

"Stay at Home Economics" by Megan Basham (Townhall.com, February 25, 2007). http://www.townhall.com/columnists/MeganBasham/2007/05/25/stay-at-home_economics.

## On Women's Happiness and Fulfillment

To say that most women have different life priorities than most men has been a highly political and incorrect fact over the last few decades. To acknowledge that most mothers prefer to work something less than full-time hours at demanding jobs or that few young women plan to spend the entirety of their adult lives in the daily grind is even more so. But many scientists and researchers are starting to confront the biological reality that women are different from men and, thus, the things that make us happy are different as well.

One of the best books to cover the issue of women's unique priorities and the genetic basis for them is by psychologist Susan Pinker. Basing her conclusions on years of clinical practice, extensive research, and personal stories, she boldly confronts the fact that what women really want out of life isn't what feminists say they should want—and that there isn't anything wrong with that.

*The Sexual Paradox: Men, Women, and the Real Gender Gap* by Susan Pinker (Scribner, 2008).

In the introduction I briefly summarized this study by Dr. W. Bradford Wilcox and Dr. Steven Nock. In it, they show that the happiest wives are those whose husbands earn at least two-thirds of the family's income.

"What's Love Got To Do With It?" by W. Bradford Wilcox and

Steven L. Nock (Social Forces, March, 2006). Visit the website outlining the study's findings at www.happiestwives.org.*

*The third most-important factor Wilcox and Nock find for women's marital happiness is a breadwinning husband: "American wives, even wives who hold more feminist views about working women and the division of household tasks, are typically happier when their husband earns 68 percent or more of the household income. Husbands who are successful breadwinners probably give their wives the opportunity to make choices about work and family—e.g., working part-time, staying home, or pursuing a meaningful but not particularly remunerative job—that allow them to best respond to their own needs, and the needs of their children.

## On Men's Happiness and Fulfillment

It can be difficult to remember in these male-bashing times, but men deserve lives filled with joy, fulfillment, and purpose just as much as women do. There aren't many books out there that concern themselves with men's welfare, but these two insightful and well-grounded entries can help you understand what motivates your husband and how to help him achieve lasting satisfaction with his work and his life.

*For Women Only: What You Need to Know About the Inner Lives of Men* by Shaunti Feldhahn (Multnomah Books, 2004).

*What Could He Be Thinking?: How a Man's Mind Really Works* by Michael Gurian (St. Martin's Griffin, 2004).

# Acknowledgments

The idea for writing about how wives contribute to their husband's careers sprung from the examples of numerous smart, successful, and affectionate couples, many of whom have appeared in this book. I'd like to thank all those who shared their stories and inspired me with their examples.

I owe quite a debt of gratitude to Stephen Hayes at *The Weekly Standard* who, by graciously answering an e-mail from a writer he'd never met, set the ball rolling. That ball then rolled to Eric Simonoff. Eric, whenever I have imagined a high-powered, New York literary agent I always pictured someone, well, nothing like you. I hear you can be a tough customer when you need to be, but the kindness and encouragement you show your clients makes it hard to believe. Thanks for seeing the potential in an unconventional subject and for being the kind of agent who wears Doc Martens with business suits.

I can't imagine what this book would be without the input of my editor Rick Horgan at Crown. Whenever I got mired down in the material, Rick gave me a guiding light of smart, incisive suggestions, and pushed me to do better work than I believed myself capable. Thanks, Rick, for your patience, enthusiasm, and for not pulling any punches. Every first-time author should have a veteran like you to team up with.

Publishing your first book can be something of a trial by fire (or at least it was for me). Every self-doubt or bad habit is magnified by it. So I'm especially grateful to the friends and family who helped me fight through insecurity, inertia, and distraction to bring this one to completion.

My dear friend and wonderful writer Sue Cameron read drafts upon drafts of this manuscript, offering invaluable insights. Our afternoons of discussion and prayer informed every page and made the whole infinitely better. If I'd had to pay someone to listen to me vent as much as Darlene Schmitt did (with the patience of Job no less), I'd be penniless. Darlene, who needs therapy when you're only a phone call away? If there is anyone who believes in the power of a wife more than I do, it is my aunt, Angela Traubel. Whenever my perseverance started to waiver, your passion renewed mine. And I am especially grateful to my wonderful in-laws Jack, Melissa, Dawn, and Jimmy. Thank you all so much for your ongoing prayers, for giving me homes away from home to get some work done, and for expressing avid interest in this project during the many months I was working on it (if you were faking it, you did a great job!).

Certainly I could not have written this book were it not for the foundation my parents, Steve and Kay Carl, gave me growing up. My father taught me that it is more important to embrace truth than trends, and my mother that bringing order and beauty to a home is not an insignificant endeavor but one that enriches your own life and those of everyone around you. That wisdom is reflected in every word.

Finally, and most important, to my husband, Brian. Though this book is about how wives help their husbands fulfill their dreams, I could write a hundred books about how you have helped me fulfill mine. My life is blessed with laughter, love, and friendship every day because I share it with you.

# INDEX

Accountemps, 125
Adams, John and Abigail, 30, 31, 215–22
advice, 69–70, 139–42, 143
adviser, wife as, 125–43, 176
alternative explanation, 113–14
Amazon.com, 86–88, 182–83
American Booksellers Association, 88
American Express, 138, 173, 175, 176
American Psychological Association, 110
American Revolution, 216–19
anxiety, 56, 95, 96, 97, 119
Arnold, Bob, 125
AskMen.com, 44
Astley-Sparke, Peter, 149–50
aural neurons, 131–32
autism, 131
axons, 72

Baird, John and Leslie, 173–76, 180–82, 194
Belkin, Lisa, 21–22
Bell, Raja, 108–10, 188
beside-every-man solution, 30–33. See also career partnership
Bezos, Jeff and MacKenzie, 85–88, 89–90, 182–83, 194

biology, 51, 83, 129–32, 140, 143, 151
Boston Globe, 103, 183
brain, 72–73, 78, 95, 116, 207
negative information and, 119–20
women's vs. men's, 103, 129–32, 140, 143
Bressler, Richard J., 78
bride price, 51
Brizendine, Louann, 130, 133
Brown, Dan, 183
Bryant, Kobe, 109
Buckingham, Marcus, 71, 76, 184–85
Bureau of Labor Statistics, 21
Bush, Laura, 163
business skills, 147, 153–69
BusinessWeek, 201
Byrne, Patrick, 161
Byrne, Rhonda, 101

Cameron, Craig and Sue, 191–94
Campbell, Dawn, 160
Campbell, Glen, 162–63
Cannistraro, John, Sr, and Rita, 185–86, 194, 203
career coach, 66–69, 74, 88, 214
career partnership, 5, 9–13, 17, 74, 91–92, 214–23
advantages of, 30–33

as collaboration, 151–52, 175–86
demands on wife of, 194
equality in, 32
evidence supporting, 37–62
famous examples of, 30, 31, 183–84, 215–22
flexibility and, 66–69, 81
game plan for, 195
husband's gratitude and, 177–78
ideal selves and, 53–61, 102
identifying own strengths and, 180–84, 195
motivation and, 95–121
networking and, 153–69, 214, 215, 219
productivity and, 187–90
resource pooling and, 184–87, 195
unasked for help and, 190–94
wife's advice and, 125–43
wife's social skills and, 128–33, 153, 159–63, 167–68
wife's unpaid role in, 176–95
Carter, Jimmy, 67
Center for Work-Life Policy, 199
CEOs, 31–32, 69, 70, 135, 161
natural strengths and, 78, 79, 82
visualizing self as, 116
wife as adviser to, 125, 127, 137–38
women as, 22
change, 83–85, 102
Chaplin, Charles, 136
cheerleading, 100–101, 110, 121
Chiklis, Michael and Michelle, 98–99, 150
child-care costs, 22, 47
childhood ambitions, 75
Chittister, Joan, 207
Chiumento, 125
Citigroup, 31–32, 138

Clifton, Donald, 184–85
collaboration. See career partnership
communication skills, 80–81, 106–7, 130–33, 147–48, 153–54
advice giving and, 139–42, 143
competence, 178–79
filling husband's gaps in, 184–87
competition, 83, 143, 151
collaboration vs., 178
confidence, 119, 135, 195
conversational style, 139–42, 147–48, 150, 159, 169
Covey, Stephen, 104
Cowan, Chuck, 43
criticism, 97, 99, 165
Cusack, John, 57–58

Daily Express, 137
Davis, Paul, 183
Dean, Howard, 163–64
Decision Analyst, 43
decisions, 125, 128, 138–39, 142
questioning of, 99–100
depression, 47, 53, 56, 96, 107, 200
Dickinson, Emily, 187
Digital Dynamics, Inc., 128
Dime Bank, 82
direct advice, 140, 141
disputing technique, 112
divorce, 28, 29
Dixie Steel (band), 162
Dr. 90210 (TV program), 18–20
Drigotas, Stephen, 53
Dunleavey, M. P., 27–28

E! (cable channel), 18
Earl Industries, 205
effort, praise for, 107–8, 121
emotional intelligence, 128–35, 138–39, 143
emotional support, 182, 189

emotional well-being, 107
employee relations, 166
encouragement, 102, 119, 121,
     192, 215
endorphins, 207
ESPN, 109–10
estrogen, 131
evolutionary psychology, 24
excellence, potential for, 72–73
explanatory styles, 110–15

failure and setbacks, 89, 105
external sources of, 112, 121
*Failure to Launch* (film), 23
faith, 99, 101, 107
Families and Work Institute, 201
Family Therapy Institute of Santa
     Barbara, 76–77
*Fantastic Four* (film), 99
fear, 101, 120, 121
Feldhahn, Shaunti, 42–45, 46, 49,
     99–100
*Feminine Brain, The* (Brizendine),
     130
feminine way of life, 3–4, 20–21
femininity, masculinity vs., 50
feminism, 23, 29, 188, 213–14
*Financial Times*, 78
flexibility factor, 66–69, 81
Ford, Gerald, 70
Ford, Richard, 183–84
Frank, Matt and Marisa, 47–49
friends, 147, 148, 150
help from, 157–58, 168, 169

Gallup, George, Jr., 42–43
Gallup Organization, 42–43, 71,
     74
Gallup poll, 71
gender differences, 50–51
     advice giving and, 140–42, 143
     attachment to work and, 41, 42–
     49

biological factors in, 51, 83,
     129–32, 140, 143
business skills and, 147, 153–69
collaboration and, 151–52, 178
communication skills and, 153–
     54
competition and, 83, 178
conversational style and, 139–
     42, 148
on feeling inadequate vs.
     unloved, 100
feminist view of, 213–14
intuition and, 127, 128–33
marriage premium and, 40–41,
     133
mate desirability and, 24–25
networking and, 150–51
risk and, 83
social circles and, 40–41, 147–
     48
social skills and, 128–33, 153,
     159–61, 167–68
stereotypes and, 183
stress response and, 151
worry propensity and, 95–97
*See also* male provider role
*Get to Work* (Hirshman), 23
Giuliani, Rudy, 78
glass ceiling, 21
goals, 117–19, 120, 157, 214
Google, 200
Gormley, Rowan and Jenny, 127,
     132–33
guilt, 49, 110, 202
Gurian, Michael, 53
gut feelings, 131

Hakins, Catherine, 24
Hallowell, Edward, 201
Haltzman, Scott, 153, 153–54
*Handbook of Emotions, The* (text),
     119
happiness, 107, 207

*Hardball* (TV program), 66, 169
hard truths, 126–27
health issues, 47, 199–200, 207
help, 152, 178–80, 199, 214
  when not asked for, 190–94, 195
Hewlett, Sylvia Ann, 199
*High Fidelity* (film), 23, 57–59
Hill, Napoleon, 101
Hindery, Leo, 78
Hirshman, Linda, 23
Hitchcock, Alfred and Alma, 30,
  31, 136–37, 183, 215
honesty factor, 126–27, 133
Hooters Tour, 188
hormones, 83, 129, 131
hotel "unplugged packages,"
  202–3
housework, 39–40

ideal self, 53–61, 102
"if only" thinking, 66
immune system, 207
income
  couple's earning ratio, 27–29, 52
  optimistic explanatory style
    and, 114–15
  quality of life and, 5, 207, 208
  single vs. married men, 39-40
    (*see also* marriage premium)
  stay-at-home wife's skills and,
    173–95
  two-income couples, 4, 7, 18, 20,
    41
  women's, 24, 25, 29, 41, 46, 47
  *See also* male provider role
industrial psychology, 79
insecurity, 29, 53, 56, 100
International Investor Institute,
  128
Internet, 85–86, 88
intuition, 128–33, 143

Jackson, Alan and Denise, 162–63

*Jay Jay the Jet Plane* (TV pro-
  gram), 77
J.C. Cannistraro Company, 185–86
Jefferson, Thomas, 219
Johnson, Zach and Kim, 188–90,
  194, 204–5, 206
*Journal of Marriage and Family,*
  17

Kennedy, John F. and Jackie, 163
King, Martin Luther, Jr., 104
King, Stephen, 183
*Knocked Up* (film), 23

Lee, Johnny, 146
leisure activities, 199–209
Levin, Gerald, 135
linear thinking, 74, 129
listening, 131–32
literary wives, 183–84
love, 29, 30, 100, 127, 179, 213,
  216, 221

MacMannis, Don and Debra, 76–
  77
male provider role, 13, 22, 26, 29–
  30, 44–53, 55–56
  wife's affirmation of, 57, 59, 60,
    61, 62
manipulation, 60, 141
"Man Laws," 202
marriage, 3–4, 5, 17–21
  expectations and, 7–9, 27, 53
  interdependence in, 213–23
  masculine maturity and, 50–53
  mating preferences and, 24–25
  primary wage-earner in, 29 (*see
    also* male provider role)
  reading husband's emotions
    and, 133–35
  strengthening of, 60
  supportiveness in, 17, 51, 182,
    189

true meaning of wife and husband in, 213–23
*See also* career partnership
*Marriage in Men's Lives* (Nock), 50
marriage premium, 38–41, 53, 94,
102, 133
masculine maturity, 50–53
masculinity, 147, 202
Masters Tournament, 189, 204
Matthews, Chris and Kathleen,
66–68, 74, 81, 85, 158–59
McCullough, David, 9–10, 216,
222
McCullough, Rosalee, 10
men
changing image of, 23–24
insecurity triggers of, 97, 99–
100
as linear thinkers, 129
masculinity and, 147, 202
maturity and, 50–53
priorities of, 44
self-esteem and, 49–50, 56
*See also* gender differences;
male provider role
men's careers, 12, 24, 56, 157
change-adverse wives and, 83–
85
game plan for, 91–92
identity linked with, 20, 41–53,
202, 205, 206
importance to wives of, 25, 26–
27
lack of direction in, 6–7, 65–66,
91
lack of motivation in, 37–38,
68–69
long-held dreams and, 92
new direction of, 68–69, 73, 91–
92
personal life and, 199–209
reinvention of image and, 98–
99

risk taking and, 67–69, 81, 83–
87
satisfaction and, 77, 84
secret fears and, 100
seeking/accepting help and,
179–80
strengths and, 69–92, 106–7
work addiction and, 199–200,
207
*See also* career partnership;
marriage premium; success
mental health, 107
Michelangelo Phenomenon, 54,
57–61, 102
Microsoft, 138
Mill, John Stuart, 183
Miller, Jerry, 205–6
Monster.com, 155
Moonves, Les, 79
Morgan, Frank and Gloria, 117–
18, 166, 215
Morgan, Gloria, 117–18, 166, 215
motivation, 53, 95–121, 129, 195
husband's lack of, 37–38, 68–69
methods of, 101–20, 214–15,
218–19
new career and, 73
wife's role in, 99–102, 121, 150,
176, 216, 221
MSNBC, 66, 67, 85, 159
Msn.com, 27

nagging, 96, 97, 99, 187
cheerleading vs., 100–101, 110
NASA, 200–201
NBA, 108, 109, 110
negativity, 96–97, 119–20, 121
help in changing, 111–12
networking, 83, 147–69, 214, 215,
219
neurons, 131–32
*New York* (magazine), 28
*New York Times*, 41, 78

*New York Times Magazine,* 21–22
Nissley, Hal and Juanita, 128–29
Nock, Steven, 50, 51, 56, 59–60
Nolen-Hoeksema, Susan, 96–97
nonverbal communication, 131
*Now, Discover Your Strengths*
 (Buckingham), 71

Obama, Barack and Michelle, 164–
 65
O'Connell, Patricia Hitchcock,
 136–37
O'Neill, Tip, 67
opportunities, 81, 84–85
explanations of missed, 113–14
optimism, 104–5, 110–20
"Opt-Out Revolution, The"
 (Belkin), 21–22
Oracle, 128
outcome-based visualization, 116,
 119
Overstock.com, 161
oxytocin, 83

paradigm shift, 104
Parsons, Laura, 69–70, 74, 82, 83,
 85, 134–35, 215
Parsons, Richard, 32, 81–82, 85,
 134–35, 139
 natural strengths of, 74, 78, 79,
 215
 transformation of, 56–57, 69–70
partner wives. *See* career partnership
part-time work, 17, 20, 21, 43, 44
PBS, 77
Peale, Norman Vincent, 104
persistence, 107–15, 176, 221
perspective, 199–209
pessimism, 96, 104, 105, 110–11,
 113, 120
 three "Ps" of, 111, 112
Pew Research Center, 21, 44, 49

PGA, 188, 189, 190, 194
Phoenix Suns, 108, 109
Pinker, Susan, 83
*Pleasure Garden, The* (O'Connell),
 136–37
politics, 66–67, 74, 163–65
partner-wives and, 30, 31, 215–22
positive image, 153, 163–65, 206–7
positive psychology, 107
positive thinking, 104, 112, 114–20
positive visualization, 115–20
PriceWaterhouseCoopers, 202
problem solving, 76, 105, 178
process-based visualization, 116,
 118–19, 120
productivity, 187–90, 200–201
provider. *See* male provider role
public relations, 147, 153–54,
 158–61, 163–69, 215, 219,
 220–21
Public Relations Society of
 America, 153

questions, 99–100, 140, 141, 143

racial barriers, 102–4
"rapport talk," 140
reading people, 128–29, 132–35,
 138–39, 143
Reitman, Frieda, 41
Reivich, Karen, 112
relocation, 48, 59, 84, 85
resentment, 7–8, 27, 53, 99, 101
respect, 28, 33, 99–100, 178, 220
risk taking, 67–69, 81, 83–90, 92,
 99
Robbins, Tony, 104
Robinson, Jackie and Rachel, 30,
 31, 102–4
Romano, Ray and Anna, 126

Saint-Exupéry, Antoine de, 222
salary. *See* income

*San Francisco Examiner,* 67
Schmitt, Perry and Darlene, 153–55
"Secret Lives of Breadwinner Wives, The" (Dunleavey), 27–28
security, 83–85
*Seinfeld* (TV series), 24
self-blame, 56
self-esteem, 49–50, 54, 56, 105
self-image, 53–54, 102
Seligman, Martin, 110–11
sexuality, 28
*Sexual Paradox, The* (Pinker), 83
*Shield, The* (TV series), 98–99, 150
shortcomings. *See* weaknesses
slacker male image, 23–24, 69
"smart dummy" system, 138–39, 143
socialization, 129, 151
social occasions, 159–61, 169
social skills
    as natural strength, 80–81, 106–7
    women's advantage in, 40–41, 128–33, 147–48, 153, 159–63, 167–68
    *See also* emotional intelligence; networking
Spane, Rocky and Linda, 166–68
spiritual side of work, 207–8
status, 140, 148, 158
stay-at-home mothers, 4–5, 20–22, 43, 44, 47–48
    financial contribution by, 173, 174–76, 188
    husband's business functions and, 159, 160
    statistics on, 21
Stewart, Martha, 4, 182
strengths, 70, 71–92
    applying, 79–82, 87, 91–92, 107, 176

emphasizing effort and, 107–8
    focusing on, 71–72
    identifying husband's, 74–79, 81–82, 91, 173, 174, 176
    identifying own, 180–84, 195
    as motivational emphasis, 73, 105–7, 121
    risk management and, 83–87
Strengthsfinder.com, 74, 91
stress, 105
stress release, 208, 215
stress response, 151
success, 125–26, 159–61, 169, 176–77, 214
    disinterest in, 37–38
    flexibility and, 66–69
    high achievers and, 71, 184–85
    motivation and, 101–4, 121
    natural talents and, 74, 121
    overwork as counterproductive to, 200, 208
    security vs., 83
    visualizing for, 115–20
synaptic connections, 72–73, 78

talents. *See* strengths
Tannen, Deborah, 139–40
testosterone, 83, 131
Time Warner, 32, 56, 69, 70, 78, 82, 135
truth-detecting skill, 131–32
Twain, Mark, 183

*USA Today,* 20
Utah Jazz, 109

vacations. *See* leisure activity
*Vanity Fair* (magazine), 164–65
Vaughn, Mo, 103
Viacom, 78
Virgin Wines, 127
visualization, 115–20, 121
volunteering, 207–8, 209

wages. *See* income
*Wall Street Journal,* 149, 151
weaknesses, 71–72, 178, 179
  compensating for husband's,
    184–87, 195
websites, 74, 85–88
Weill, Joan, 137–38, 214–15
Weill, Sandy, 31–32, 137–38
Weiss, Robert S., 45–46, 49, 56,
  178
Wilcox, W. Bradford, 29
Winfrey, Oprah, 21
women
  bonding among, 147–48
  intrinsic priorities of, 83
  male model of achievement
    and, 123–24
  needs of, 29–30
  networking ability of, 147–69
  pooling resources among, 158
  public relations skills of, 147,
    153–69

  unique value of, 125–43
  *See also* gender differences
women's careers, 25, 147
  career partnership vs., 173–95
  compartmentalizing of, 49
  disenchantment with, 4, 20–23,
    43, 44
  exit strategy and, 23, 48
  husband's view of, 46–47
  marriage premium and, 40–41,
    133
  preferences and, 17, 21
  public relations as, 153–54
  using skills learned from, 30,
    31, 173, 175–78, 180–81
Woods, Tiger, 189
work addiction, 199–200, 207
work benefits package, 200
worry, 95–97, 98, 115–16, 179
Wylie, Frank, 153

# ABOUT THE AUTHOR

MEGAN BASHAM has written for numerous publications, including *The Weekly Standard and American Spectator,* and her work has been either referenced or excerpted in such publications as *The Wall Street Journal* and the *Los Angeles Times.* She is also an in-demand on-air commentator.